FROM **TRIUMPH** TO **TRAGEDY** IN THE **NHL**

Brad J. Lombardo

Copyright © 2015 by Brad J. Lombardo

Published 2015 by Brad J. Lombardo
Richmond Hill, ON Canada

All rights reserved. No part of this publication may be reproduced, stored in a retrieval system or transmitted, in any form or by any means, electronic, mechanical, photocopying, recording or otherwise, without prior permission of the publisher.

This book is sold subject to the condition that it shall not by way of trade or otherwise, be lent, resold, hired out, or otherwise circulated without the publisher's prior consent in any form of binding or cover other than that in which it is published and without a similar condition including this condition being imposed on the subsequent purchaser.

Photographs courtesy of the D.K. (Doc) Seaman Hockey Resource Centre, a division of the Hockey Hall of Fame.

Photo Credits:
Steve Chiasson, Dave Sandford/Hockey Hall of Fame
Pelle Linbergh, O-Pee-Chee/Hockey Hall of Fame
John Kordic, Paul Bereswill/Hockey Hall of Fame
Terry Sawchuk, O-Pee-Chee/Hockey Hall of Fame
Bill Masterton, Graphic Artists/Hockey Hall of Fame
Tim Horton, Imperial Oil, Turofsky/Hockey Hall of Fame

Book Design: Pat Carito/Creative Director
Rebrand Advertising and Design Inc.

ISBN-13: 978-1493709052
ISBN-10: 1493709054

Printed in the United States by CreateSpace
First Edition

Special discounts for bulk quantities of this book are avaialble to corporations, institutions, associations and other organizations.

For more information contact us at bradlombardo@rogers.com or garcialorcaengranada@gmail.com

CONTENTS

ACKNOWLEDEMENTS   **5**

PREFACE   **6**

1. BILL MASTERTON   **8**

    In 1967 the NHL expanded from six to twelve teams, allowing this career minor leaguer to finally make the big league, with the Minnesota North Stars. Early in the 1968-69 season, in a game against the Oakland Seals and at just twenty-nine years of age, Masterton suffered severe brain trauma; the rookie forward eventually succumbed to his injuries.

2. TERRY SAWCHUK   **24**

    Arguably hockey's greatest goaltender, he was a four-time winner of both the Stanley Cup and the Vezina Trophy, the latter for best goalie. Often injured, Sawchuk managed to play for twenty-one seasons, with Detroit, Boston, Toronto, Los Angeles and New York. In the summer of 1970 the forty-year-old died in the hospital of stomach injuries.

3. TIM HORTON   **54**

    One of the premier defensemen from the Original Six era, this sturdy rearguard was rock solid for twenty-four seasons with Toronto, Pittsburgh, New York and Buffalo. During the 1973-74 season Horton was killed after crashing his sports car late at night; the forty-four year old was driving home, after being named third star in a game at Maple Leaf Gardens.

4. PELLE LINDBERGH   76

The first European goalie to capture the Vezina Trophy, Lindbergh was a star in the making and the answer to the Philadelphia Flyer's prayers. Early in the 1985-86 season he suffered severe brain injuries after crashing his sports car late at night; just twenty-four years of age, he was taken off life support soon after.

5. JOHN KORDIC   94

This troubled enforcer was just a rookie when he won the Cup with Montreal. Kordic wore out his welcome there, and ended up with Quebec, after stints in Toronto and Washington. In the summer of 1992 the thirty-two year old bad boy died after a prolonged physical scuffle with Quebec City police; alcohol and drug use were also involved.

6. STEVE CHIASSON   122

An all-star in 1993, this dependable and physical defenseman punished opposing forwards for eight seasons, with Detroit, Calgary, Hartford and Carolina. Chiasson attended a team party after his Hurricanes were ousted from the 1999 Stanley Cup playoffs, but on the way home the thirty-one year old crashed his pick-up truck and was killed instantly.

END NOTES   140

PLAYER STATISTICS   152

FROM TRIUMPH TO TRAGEDY IN THE NHL

ACKNOWLEDGEMENTS

There were many resources which I found valuable as I researched this book, including some informative, well-written books on former NHLers Terry Sawchuk (Dennis Dupuis and Brian Kendall), Tim Horton (Douglas Hunter) and John Kordic (Mark Zwolinski). I wish to thank each of these authors; their sources were quite comprehensive and insightful, and enabled me to better understand the lives of these hockey players.

Other research material was also very relevant to my research, including various books, magazine articles, and/or newspaper stories written by, among others, Eric Adelson, Stephen Cole, Damien Cox, Bob Duff, Stan Fischler, Howard Liss, Brian MacFarlane, Henry Roxborough, Jon Scher, and the late Dick Beddoes, Trent Frayne, and Scott Young.

I offer further appreciation to former NHLers interviewed while researching for this endeavor, including Ben Woit, Johnny Bower, and the now deceased Lorne Gump Worsley.

I wish to also thank my wife Margaret and daughter Vanessa, as well as all my other family and friends for their continual encouragement and support; a special mention goes to Consultant Editor Salvatore Ala for his editing contributions, and to Associate Editor Rob Osborne for his creative ideas.

This book is dedicated with sincere gratefulness and love to my parents, William Secondo Lombardo and Jina Maria Innocente Lombardo, both of whom are now deceased but remain dearly missed.

PREFACE

Growing up in Windsor, Ontario in the 1960s, I read just about every hockey book penned by the late sportswriter Scott Young, and I also dreamed of someday writing my own. By the mid-1970s my parents had moved with their three youngest children, myself included, to southern Spain, but my passion for the national game never abated. Our family returned to Windsor in the 1980s, and soon after I briefly worked as a sportswriter, first in Windsor and later on in Montreal. For almost two decades I have been teaching in the Greater Toronto Area, and in recent years have had the opportunity to develop this manuscript.

The original idea was to profile the professional careers and personal lives of NHL players who died tragically, while in pursuit of their pro careers. While I eventually focused on the six hockey players in this book, my initial research included early American college hockey star Hobey Baker, as well as pioneering NHL legends Georges Vezina, Charlie Gardiner, Howie Morenz, and Bill Barilko.

I also found insightful information on the careers and lives of other NHL players who had died in the midst of their playing careers, including: Frank McGee, Joe Hall, Jack Darragh, Babe Siebert, Red Garrett, Joe Turner, Michel Briere, Bob Gassof, Yanick Dupre, Stephane Morin, Dmitri Tertyshny, Roman Lyashenko, Dan Snyder, Derek Boogard, Mark Rypien, and Steve Montador. Also remembered is the 2011 Lokomotiv Yaroslavl air disaster, which claimed the lives of almost an entire team from the KHL in Russia. Former NHLers on that doomed flight were Pavol Demitra, Alexander Karpovtsev, Igor Korolev, Brad McCrimmon, and Ruslan Salei.

Steve Chiasson

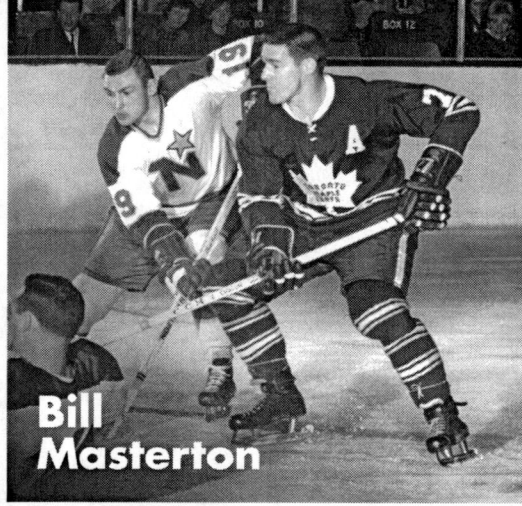

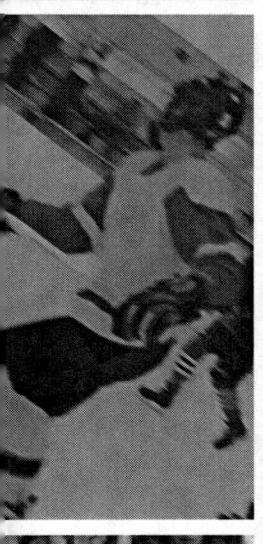

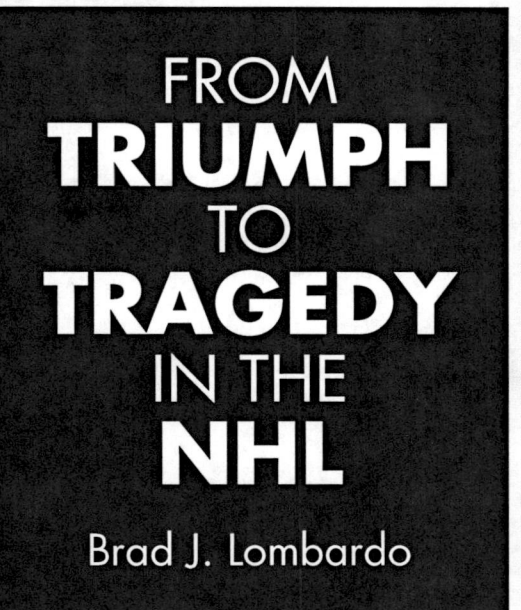

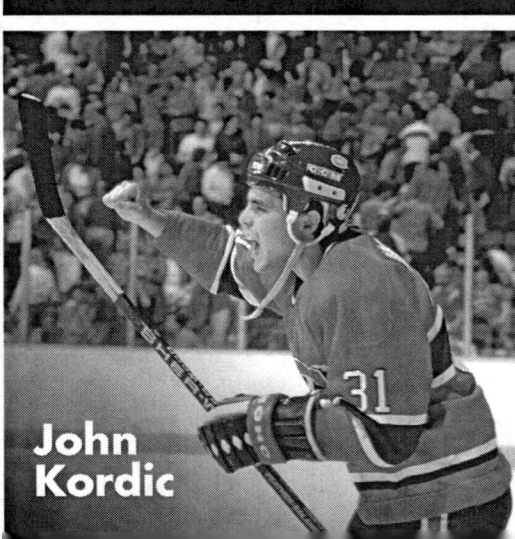

Bill Masterton

Terry Sawchuk

FROM TRIUMPH TO TRAGEDY IN THE NHL

Brad J. Lombardo

Pelle Lindbergh

John Kordic

Tim Horton

8

CHAPTER 1

1938 - 1968

BILL MASTERTON

In 1967 former American College Star Bill Masterton finally realized his dream of playing in the NHL. The 29-year-old Masterton suited up for the expansion-team Minnesota North Stars to start the regular season, an unproven rookie at an age when many pro players were either established NHLers or resigned to finishing their careers in the minors. Providing the North Stars with much-needed poise at the center position, Masterton soon became one of the team's better forwards. Tragedy struck on January 13, 1968, however, when Bill suffered severe head injuries during a game against the Oakland Seals. He died in the hospital just a day later, and his demise remains the only fatality in NHL history resulting directly from on-ice play.

GROWING UP IN WINNIPEG

Born August 13, 1938 in Winnipeg, Manitoba, young Bill Masterton dreamed of an NHL career, often developing his hockey skills on the city's frozen ponds. He played defense in midget and bantam, but his deft moves with the puck were more like those of a crafty young center. Every Saturday evening in the small Masterton home in Winnipeg's East Kildonan district, brothers Bill and Bob listened to Foster Hewitt broadcast hockey on the radio. "We spent a lot of time dreaming," recalled Bob. "But my brother was the worker and had the ethic you need to make the NHL."

Eventually switching to the pivot position, at 17 he joined the St. Boniface Canadiens of the Manitoba Junior Hockey League (MJHL). In just 22 games Masterton managed 23 goals and 49 points, leading the team in scoring, and added another six points in the playoffs. St. Boniface advanced to the Memorial Cup Finals, where Bill posted eight points and was the Canadiens' dominant forward.

His sophomore season with St. Boniface was even more impressive, as he led the team in scoring again, with 53 points, and added another 18 points in the playoffs. Bill's ten assists led all playoff scorers that year, his stellar play soon catching the attention of scouts from the University of Denver, who offered him a hockey scholarship.

A STAR IN AMERICAN COLLEGE HOCKEY

Accepting the offer, the 19-year-old Masterton entered the University of Denver in the fall of 1957, intent on pursuing an undergraduate degree in Business Studies. As a freshman he focused on academic studies, forgoing a place on the school hockey team, the Pioneers of the Western Collegiate Hockey Association (WCHA). He joined the squad the following year and never looked back, scoring 21 goals and 49 points in just 23 games as he helped the Pioneers advance to the NCAA championship tournament, where they won the collegiate title.

The following season Bill compiled 67 points and was selected to the WCHA's First All-Star Team as well as the First All-American Team of the NCAA West (National Collegiate of Amateur Athletics). Again, he helped the Pioneers capture the collegiate championship. By the 1960-61 campaign Masterton had developed into U.S. College hockey's top offensive player; he repeated his all-star selection honours, repeated as team scoring leader and led his Pioneers to a third collegiate title. The dominant offensive force in the finals, for his efforts he was selected tournament MVP and also made the NCAA Championship All-American team.[1]

ADVANCING THRU THE PRO RANKS

In the fall of 1961 Bill graduated with a Bachelor degree in Business Administration from the University of Denver, and then decided to turn pro after signing a contract with the NHL's Montreal Canadiens. "I signed with the Montreal organization and was assigned to their Hull-Ottawa farm club in the Eastern Professional Hockey League (for 1961-62)," he later recalled.

"After scoring 31 goals and 35 assists there, I was moved up to Cleveland (of the American Hockey League) the following season and had what I thought was a pretty good year."[2] Masterton finished sixth in AHL scoring in 1962-63 notching 82 points in 72 games with the AHL Barons. He added another 9 points in the playoffs, but the Barons fell short in their quest for the Calder Cup.

Masterton had produced offensively during his stints in the EPHL and AHL, but the prospects of advancing through Montreal's organizations seemed remote. "The Canadiens were loaded with centers," he later recollected, "so I really never had much of a chance to make the grade with them."[3] Left unprotected by the Habs in the 1963 waiver draft, Bill decided to quit pro hockey and concentrate on his education when no other NHL club picked him up.

He was re-instated as an amateur, and in the fall of that year enrolled in a graduate studies program at the University of Denver. Having completed his Master's degree in Finance in early 1964, Masterton was busy preparing himself for a professional business career. "By that time I had gotten married," he later remembered, "and there was this offer to work in contract administration for a big, established firm like Honeywell. Everything seemed to be working out so well, I really didn't have much time to think about hockey."[4]

PERSISTENCE PAYS OFF

Bill never completely abandoned his dream of playing pro hockey. He continued to play amateur hockey in the United States while working for Honeywell, and returned to pro hockey for the 1964-65 season when he joined the Rochester Mustangs of the United States Hockey League. He remained in the USHL the following season and tallied 67 points in just 30 points for the St. Paul Steers, his 40 assists tops in the league. He played several exhibition games for the U.S. National Team in 1966-67, compiling 39 points in 21 games. Pro scout Wren Blair attended several of the games, and became increasingly impressed with the centre's strong two-way play.

Like other aspiring minor league hockey talents, Masterton's hopes of one day playing in the NHL had received a huge boost with the announcement in 1965 that the NHL planned to expand by the 1967-68 campaign, doubling its size to 12 teams. The new entries were the Los Angeles Kings, Minnesota North Stars, Oakland Seals, Philadelphia Flyers, Pittsburgh Penguins and St. Louis Blues. Expansion led to a huge increase in the number of NHL jobs open to hockey players, and afforded a golden opportunity to a lot of career minor leaguers, such as Masterton.

The newly established Minnesota North Stars hockey club hired Wren Blair as Coach and General Manager. As a member of the Boston Bruins' management nucleus in the mid -1960s, Blair had a penchant for discovering talented young players, and was largely responsible for his club's adroit drafting of young Bobby Orr. Already impressed with Masterton, Blair decided to act.

> I liked what I saw so I asked Bill if he would consider giving pro hockey another fling," Blair remembered. "When he said he would like to try it, I bought his contract from Montreal.[5]

Masterton later claimed that the chance to play in the Twin Cities Area (St. Paul-Minneapolis) was an important factor, as he was familiar with the area from his short stint with the St. Paul Steers. "I doubt very much," he admitted, "whether I would've considered playing hockey any other place."[6]

Bob Masterton recalls his brother telling him about the NHL offer over dinner. "I looked at him and said, 'What are you going to do,' because he was just starting a young family," Bob said. "It was kind of one of those things where I asked the question, but I knew what he was going to do. It was always in the back of his mind."[7]

Having purchased the rights to Masterton from the Habs in June 1966, Blair signed the journeyman forward and goalie Carl Wetzel to the first two player contracts for the North Stars.[7] Initially Blair was going to put Masterton on defense, where Minnesota lacked experience and depth. This was reflective of a popular trend among all the new NHL entries in 1966 and 1967, since those first-year teams wanted to sign up as many amateur defenseman as possible. This strategy would preclude the expansion clubs from having to use hard cash to purchase farm clubs, to act as feeders for the NHL units. Cash flow was somewhat limited for all the new organizations, already burdened with unforeseen overhead costs. Purchasing farm clubs was seen as more of a long-term plan.

A ROOKIE – AT 29

When Masterton arrived at the North Stars training camp just prior to the start of the 1967-68 season, Wren Blair was still not quite sure if the player should be slotted at center or defense. Bill was anxious to make the team.

> "I went to training camp knowing it wouldn't be a picnic, especially after being out of pro hockey for four seasons," he later told reporters, "I had the opportunity to skate quite a bit last summer when I coached in a summer league, and I think that helped me quite a bit. I was in pretty good shape when I reported.[8]

One of the most impressive players at camp, he showed offensive potential and was strong defensively. Blair decided to keep the playmaker at center. Suffering a separated shoulder just before the exhibition schedule, Bill rehabbed hard to overcome the nagging injury before the start of the regular season. He was thankful to be in the lineup for the first game. He perceived it as his personal reward for all the hard work he had put into becoming a pro hockey player, particularly since his previous pro experience had precluded him from a spot on the 1968 U.S. Olympic Hockey Team.

One thing that did not follow Masterton to the NHL was the helmet that he had steadfastly adorned throughout his college hockey career. He had worn it during camp but it was still a rarity in an age when head protection was routinely dismissed, even frowned upon, by players and management alike. In Minnesota the only player to challenge the status quo and don a helmet had been Andre Boudrais and he was traded the following season. "We were not allowed to wear a helmet," recalled the late North Star winger J.P. Parise. "You would get traded if you did. It was a no-no in on uncertain terms. You were a yellow belly if you wore a helmet."[9] Masterton's head gear disappeared once he reached the NHL.

Minnesota played its first NHL regular season game on October 11, 1967, facing off against the St. Louis Blues on their home rink, the Metropolitan Sports Center. Early in the first period, Masterton took a pass in the slot, pivoted to his left, and then deftly fired a shot over the shoulder of Blues' goalie Glenn Hall, the future Hall of Famer. Masterton had scored the game's first goal, the first regular season marker ever potted by a North Star. It marked a promising start to his NHL career, and soon after he discussed his prospects of remaining in the league.

> When I signed a two-year contract, I more or less expected to spend this season at Memphis (in the minors)," he admitted. "I still may end up there but even if I do, I won't be disappointed because I've given myself two years to prove that I can play in the NHL. I realize it's going to be tough, but if I get the opportunity to play, I'm confident that I can make it.[10]

Impressed by the center's strong early showing, Blair never considered sending him down to the minors. "From what I saw of Bill in training camp, I think he'll help us," the coach reasoned, very early in the season. "He had the misfortune of getting a shoulder separation just before the exhibition games started, but he worked hard with Lloyd Percival, our physical fitness expert, and was able to return for our last six or seven games and got three goals and a couple of assists."[11]

Masterton acquitted himself well on the ice in the early going, playing strong positional hockey and winning important face-offs at both ends of the ice. An important force in the North Star's strong start, by January he was ninth in team scoring, with four goals and seven assists. The future looked bright for the rookie center as the North Stars prepared for a game at home on January 11, against the Oakland Seals.

TRAGEDY ON THE ICE

Minnesota was eager to secure its playoff position against Oakland, one of the weakest of the six expansion teams comprising the newly established Western

Division. With the top four first-year teams advancing to the 1968 Stanley Cup Playoffs, the North Stars wanted to put some distance in the standings between themselves and the Seals. Oakland was trying to climb back into the playoff race, however, and played an energetic, hard-hitting game. Early in the first period, Masterton wheeled into the Seals' defensive zone with the puck, then backhanded a pass to his linemate, right winger Wayne Connelly. He apparently lost his balance after relaying the puck, and awkwardly fell backwards, hitting the back of his head against the ice.

There are conflicting versions as to how Masterton lost his balance. Some accounts have insisted that Masterton simply lost his bearings as he executed an awkward pass, while other reports have held that he was actually hit hard by two Oakland defenseman beforehand.[12] Blair said that he was talking to one of his players on the bench when the accident occurred. "I looked up and it looked like he (Bill) collided with Ronnie Harris and then rolled off Larry Cahan before he hit the ice," he noted. "I didn't see it but some of the guys said they saw blood before his head hit the ice."[13]

Gordon Ritz, then the North Stars' Director, was at the game but did not fully see the play develop. "I didn't see it happen. I was following the puck, like everyone else, and then I heard this terrible thud when his head hit the ice," he recalled. "He and Harris had crashed together. It's a terrible shock. He wasn't a good skater but Bill was the type of kid who always gave up 140 per cent."[14] Some sportswriters who actually saw the game contended that Masterton somehow slipped or had his skates knocked out from under him in a crowd of players high-sticking each other, some 25 feet in front of the Seals' net.[15] Another account of the incident asserts that Masterton regained consciousness for a few moments and repeated the words "never again, never again" before closing his eyes for the final time.

NHL President Clarence Campbell later noted to the press that referee Wally Harris never called a penalty on the play. "I got it second hand from the referee the same as everybody else. There was no suggestion of anything but a routine accident," he said. "His feet went out from under him and he landed on the back of his head. He had dumped the puck into the attacking zone and was chasing it."[16]

The critically-injured Masterton lay on the ice unconscious after the incident, blood seeping from his head and nose. Emergency aid was immediately given to Bill by team physician Dr. Charles Kelly and trainers Stan Waylett and Al Scheueman. The crowd at the Met was silent, obviously concerned that Masterton was seriously hurt. No response was forthcoming from Masterton, so Dr. Kelly ordered him removed on a stretcher to the dressing room. Once there, Minneapolis neurosurgeon Dr. Paul Blake joined three other physicians as they furiously worked to save the player's life.

Having detected only faint signs of life, the doctors promptly decided to have Bill rushed to nearby Fairview Southdale Hospital. Placed in intensive care, he was worked on by a team of five physicians, led by Dr. Lyle French, chief neurosurgeon of the University of Minnesota Hospitals. His brain and head injuries were so severe, however, that doctors elected not to operate and he never regained consciousness. Masterton's parents and other family members flew in from Winnipeg to see him in the hospital, and to offer much needed emotional support to his wife and children.[17]

Masterton's death in the early morning hours of January 13, less than two days after the tragic incident, shocked the hockey world. Minnesota North Stars President Walter Bush issued a team statement to the press. "I've lost a person I valued as a friend as well as one of the finest players in our organization," he said. "Bill certainly exemplified the type of person I would want my children to become. The sympathy of the North Stars goes out to Carol Masterton and to all members of Bill's family."[18]

North Stars' coach Wren Blair was particularly distraught over Masterton's demise, perhaps feeling guilty over having convinced the veteran to return to pro hockey. Perhaps inadvertently, he added to the controversy surrounding the incident by telling the press that the centre was suffering from headaches before the game, and that "he looked like he was out of it" before his head hit the ice. "You've heard of players getting killed in car accidents? At first the cause of death is reported to be because of the accident. But sometimes they later find out he suffered a heart attack," Blair noted. "I'm not saying this is what happened here, but who knows what goes on inside a person's body? To me he looked hurt before he hit the ice. He had been complaining of headaches to the guys for a few weeks now, but he didn't say anything to me.

We've had so much flu going around I guess nobody thought anything of it. He looked okay to me."[19] Masterton also absorbed a very heavy hit in a game against Boston on December 30th, the North Stars' coach noted, but seemed alright afterwards. Other spectators at the game also noted that Masterton seemed unconscious before he hit the ice, an impression they received from the particular way he fell.

Memorial services for Bill Masterton Jr. were arranged by O'Halloran and Murphy Funeral Homes of St. Paul, and were held in the Minneapolis area. Family and friends included Carol and her children, Bill's parents and his brother, Robert, who had flown in from San Diego. Also paying their respects were the North Stars players and management, as well as representatives from the other 11 NHL teams.

1968 NHL ALL-STAR GAME – IN MEMORY OF BILL MASTERTON

Each season the All-Star Game allows the NHL to showcase its top stars in a fast-spaced, entertaining affair. Held in Toronto in 1968, the event was to be particularly special, since it would be the last one pitting an all-star selection against the defending Stanley Cup champs, in this case the Maple Leafs. There was a lot sadness surrounding the game, however, since it was being played on January 16, just one day after Masterton's tragic death. Most NHLers were still disconcerted that an on-ice injury directly led to a fellow player's demise. The NHL Player's Pension Fund donated $60,000 to Carol Masterton, and all-star festivities proceeded in a subdued manner.

Prior to the all-star game there was some talk about staging a special contest in Masterton's memory, with proceeds going to his family, but Campbell clarified the matter. "There has never been a benefit game since I came into the league. I think a benefit game is asking the public to pay for a normal hazard of our business," the NHL's top executive declared. "It is our responsibility to pay indemnification wherever it is necessary. You can't compensate for a man's life, no matter what you do. This is just a built-in hazard of our business."[20]

Discussions during the pre-game festivities focused less on the stars, and more on the fiery debate about protective helmets. There were those who argued that helmets should be mandatory for players and that safety should come first, even if it means that ability and performance might be compromised. Others countered that helmets adversely impact on an NHLer's play, and that severe head injuries were not frequent enough to warrant such significant change. Maple Leafs President Stafford Smythe declared that all players should wear one, and Bobby Hull said he would consider it. "No, I won't wear a helmet," admitted Red Wing star Gordie Howe, "but I would recommend youngsters wear them."[21]

Howe's linemate, Frank Mahovlich, said he would wear one if he was ordered to do so by the league, but again NHL President Clarence Campbell let his views be known. "I don't believe regimentation is necessary," he claimed. "I think they (the players) should be encouraged to wear them, but I don't believe most players in the next generation will have learned to play with helmets."[22] He later noted that there will always be some players who want helmets. "The very best ones that money can buy are made available to the teams if the players want them. It's an optional thing," he asserted. "It was tried at one time in 1933 to make it compulsory to wear them but it was a dismal failure. Some players just don't wear them."[23] Masterton himself played with a helmet in U.S. College hockey, as regulations required him to do, but then neglected to wear one in the NHL. Campbell also added that most NHLers are skilled players who rarely lose their balance on the ice, thus avoiding the danger of serious head injuries.

At the pre-game dinner, held at the Royal York Hotel, the NHL President did not want to add to the controversy, and paid his respects to Masterton only briefly, noting how the late North Star rookie had realized his dream of playing in the NHL.[24] The NHL Writer's Association hosted a brunch on the day of the game, however, and it was decided that an honorary trophy be made for the NHL, in Bill's memory. The Writer's Association submitted a formal suggestion to the league a few weeks later, and it was immediately accepted.

There was also some history made during the game itself, a 4-3 win by Toronto. Brian Conacher of the Maple Leafs and J.C. Tremblay of the Canadiens became the first two players to wear a helmet during an all-star contest. It was a first for Conacher, who continued to wear the protective headgear for the rest of his career, but Tremblay had played with a helmet all year.

Several other NHL players, including many North Stars, started wearing helmets once the season resumed, fully realizing that they too could be seriously injured. The example was first set by such stars as Red Berenson of the St. Louis Blues and Stan Mikita of the Chicago Black Hawks. Mikita eventually convinced two of his teammates, Pit Martin and Ken Wharham, to put them on. Most players were no so inclined, however, particularly since helmets tended to be crudely made at the time. They were considered to be both uncomfortable and a hindrance to one's play. Led by Campbell, the NHL did not exactly push the issue, and it would be many years before most players had them on, even longer before they were mandatory.

The North Stars were never quite the same team after the tragedy. With many of Bill's teammates still struggling to overcome their grief, Minnesota lost six straight right after the all-star break. Having started the season on such a bright note, the North Stars barely made the playoffs, finishing fourth in the Western Division. With the players dedicating their 1968 playoffs run to Masterton, Minnesota defeated the Los Angeles Kings in the opening round. The North Stars were no match for St. Louis, however, with the Blues star goaltenders Glen Hall and Jacques Plante having led the club to first overall in the Western Division. St. Louis defeated Minnesota to advance to the Stanley Cup finals, where they lost to the Boston Bruins.

THE LEGACY: HOCKEY'S ONLY ON-ICE FATALITY

The protective equipment worn by pro hockey players had changed little during the decades leading up to Masterton's death, and only a handful of NHL players had ever donned helmets before then. It is surprising that there were not any serious injuries or deaths resulting from on-ice play before 1968, particularly considering that players remained unprotected for so long. After the tragedy, critics of the sports started demanding more vigorously that the use of protective headgear become immediately mandatory in the NHL and other pro hockey leagues. It was well into the 1990s, however, before helmets became mandatory equipment.

A significant part of Masterton's legacy will always be that his death brought changes to the game of pro hockey, eventually leading to the use of better protective equipment. In the 1960s sports journalists were often critical of the brutality and violence of hockey, and Masterton's death crystallized that perception. Such criticisms eventually had a positive impact on hockey, since the NHL and other pro leagues passed legislation for more protective equipment while working to reduce needless on-ice violence.

Shortly after his death in 1968, Bill Masterton was remembered by the North Stars in a special pre-game ceremony. A giant banner displaying his jersey number, 19, was raised from the rafters at the Metropolitan Sports Center. After the end of the season, the NHL executive made good on the request from the Writer's Association, establishing an individual award in the late player's memory. The Bill Masterton Memorial Trophy was created, to be awarded each year to the NHL player best exemplifying perseverance, dedication, and sportsmanship to hockey. The first recipient of the award, in 1968-69, was Chicago's Pit Martin, one of the few players who then wore a helmet. Perhaps it was fitting that Martin was the inaugural winner, since he was one those NHLers who helped establish the trend towards safer protective headgear. In essence, that is the lasting legacy which Masterton's tragic demise left on pro hockey.

THE TORONTO STAR INVESTIGATION

By 2011 it had been over 40 years since Masterton's tragic death and discussions were rampant in the media about the negative implications of head hits and injuries in pro hockey, such as repeated concussions and headaches, head trauma and even short-term and long-term memory loss.

In May of that year The Toronto Star reported on the results of its retroactive investigation into Masterton's death. The newspaper discovered that the North Star journeyman had been experiencing severe headaches well before his final game and was likely already suffering a concussion before his final fall.[25] According to the article, the irony is that the player's own dogged perseverance probably precipitated his untimely demise.

The Star's investigation centered on what happened in the days leading up to that fatal moment in Minneapolis, when Bill played his thirty-eighth and final NHL game. Uncovered evidence indicates that an earlier, untreated concussion was likely responsible for his death, with that injury compounded by the unwritten and time-honored hockey code among players – resilience in the face of pain, serious injury, perhaps even brain trauma.

> "I've never said this to anyone before," conceded Wren Blair, Masterton's former NHL coach, at the age of 85. "I've never thought that it had anything to do with that hit. I think he had a (pre-existing) brain hemorrhage.[26]

The newspaper also quoted others close to the journeyman who agreed that he suffered from a brain injury before the fatal game; Mavis Maniago, the wife of then-Minnesota goalie Cesar Maniago, had a direct view of Masterton's fall from her seat in the stands. She also believed that there was something wrong with Masterton just before being felled by what seemed like a routine bodycheck. "I saw Bill's head after he was just checked from behind and it just looked like his eyes were in the back of his head," she recalled. "I thought he was out then and just went fast right down."[27]

The night before that last match against Oakland, Bill was at Maniago's home with his family, helping the goalie celebrate a birthday. "He had been complaining of headaches," Maniago recollected. "He'd got hit and even that night he said, 'Gee, I've really been getting these migraines and they've been with me for about a week.'" There were also something that Wren Blair noticed several games prior. "I'd said to our trainer, 'Do you notice something with Bill when the game's on,'" Blair said. "His face is blood red, almost purple. (The trainer) said, 'Yeah, I notice that too,' I said, 'I wonder if we could have him checked. There's something wrong.'"[28] Masterton, always quick to shrug off injury, was never sent to a doctor.

Carl Johnson was assistant general manager of Minnesota's farm team in Memphis at the time; he recalled being told that Masterton had blacked out while on line rushes in practice. Memphis coach John Muckler saw signs of trouble in training camp. "I really believe he was injured before the fatal blow," argued Muckler. "I know that in our training camp he got hit hard a copy of times. And he got hit a few games very hard at the NHL level. His aggressiveness got him. He wasn't the most talented guy in the world but he wanted to play…he wanted it very badly. I've seen a person work so hard. He'd never show when he got hurt. He never laid down."[29]

Although the 1968 autopsy report surmised that Bill Masterton likely died of cerebral contusions sustained from a fall on the nice, a noted Toronto neurosurgeon and concussion expert believed that there was more to the story. Dr. Charles Tatar argued that Masterton suffered "second impact syndrome", a rare occurrence when a second concussion happens soon after a first one that has not healed properly, thus causing contusion and severe brain swelling. "We know the second hit can be fatal. The usual story is just as has unfolded here, that they can even talk a bit after that final hit and then they lapse into a coma," Tatar explained. "There is evidence of massive brain swelling…that is out of proportion to the blow that he got. My interpretation is that the seeds of this catastrophic injury were sown days before."

When journeymen like Masterston were toiling in the NHL during the old regime, all too often they played through or even hid their injuries, even if it possibly involved brain trauma, largely for fear of losing their jobs. "Injury really wasn't of any importance in the sense that you did not want to lose your job and if you couldn't play, obviously they had to fill the roster," argued former NHLer Mike Walton. "It (the hockey club) was a dictatorship. They had total control."[30] Although knowledge and treatment of concussions and other brain ailments has improved dramatically since the late 1960s, the modern hockey player still maintains that warrior-like attitude, which largely features hiding or playing through a variety of physical ailments.

Scott Masterton has always believed that his father's fate was sealed before his final game. "My mother, before she died, talked about it. He was having some headaches. My feeling is that he may have gotten a minor concussion playing or practicing on some other day," Scott reasoned, "(and) when he got hit on the head the second time, he had that head whip and when that happens, you can go unconscious in that split second before you fall."[31] A former U.S. kickboxing champion, Scott's own competitive career ended with severe injuries suffered in the ring on January 15th, the anniversary of his father's death. Scott was 29, the same age that Bill Masterton was when he died.

In the 1970s and 1980s the memory of Bill Masterton lingered with the Minnesota North Stars franchise and his former teammates and coaches. By 1991, however, the franchise was in dire straits and even changed its name from North Stars to Stars for the final two seasons in Minnesota, foreshadowing an eventual move south. In 1993 the franchise re-located to Dallas, Texas and five years later won the Stanley Cup as the Dallas Stars. The following year the NHL added two new franchises, including the Minnesota Wild, thus welcoming back the city where Bill Masterton played.

Bill Masterton is gone but not forgotten, of course, and there remain several poignant reminders of the man: the jersey hanging from the rafters of the old Met Center, the plaques bearing his name, the statues in his image, the major NHL trophy, still awarded each year in a league which eventually embraced, and then made mandatory, the donning of helmets by its players. That's not a bad legacy for a rookie 29-year-old forward who finally got the chance to chase his dream at the highest level of hockey but died too young doing it.

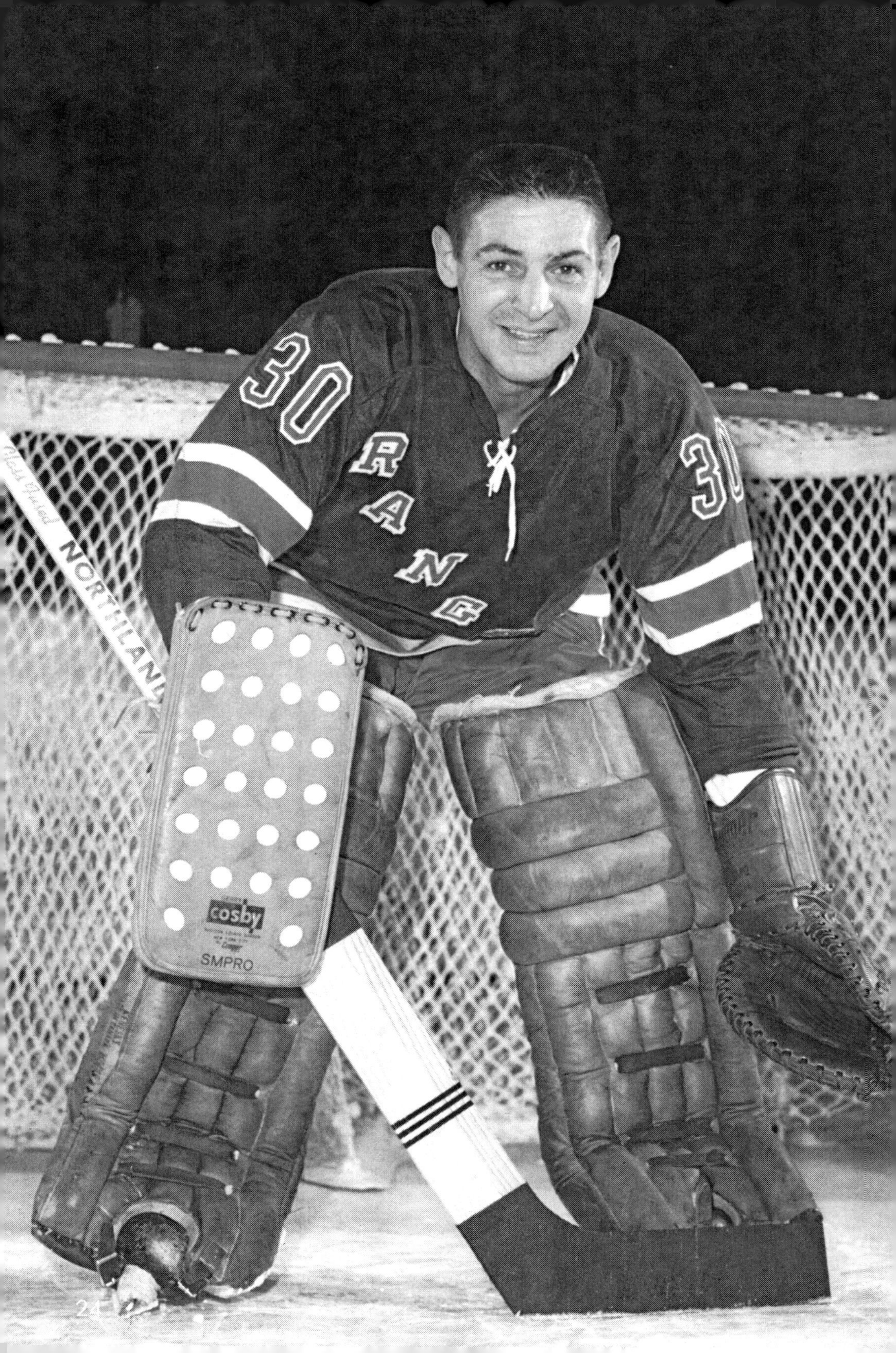
30
RANG
30
NORTHLAN
cosby
SMPRO

CHAPTER 2

1929 - 1970

TERRY SAWCHUK

The sad memorial service was held on June 5, 1970 at La Salette Catholic Church in Berkely, Michigan. Over 200 people paid their respects to the late Terry Sawchuk, arguably hockey's greatest goaltender. The 40-year-old netminding great had recently died unexpectedly in a New York area hospital, as a result of ailments from a severe stomach injury. Sawchuk had registered a then-record 103 regular season shutouts in 21 NHL seasons, for Detroit, Boston, Toronto, Los Angeles and New York. An adept innovator in the game, he had revolutionized hockey goaltending with his famous crouch style and remarkable agility and cat-like reflexes. Greatness came at a huge cost to the oft-injured star, who was gradually physically and mentally worn down over the years. Terry's death demise may not have been a complete surprise, given his past ailments, but his tragic passing was still a tremendous blow to the pro hockey world.

PRODIGY FROM MANITOBA

Terrence Gordon Sawchuk was born December 28, 1929 in East Kildonan, Manitoba, a northern working class suburb across the Red River from Winnipeg. His parents, Louis and Anne, were traditional Austrian immigrants, and his father worked as a tinsmith. As the third son, Terry grew up in the shadow of older brother Mitch, seven years his senior, who played goal in the local hockey leagues. He was taught how to skate at age four by his uncle, Nick Maslak, who encouraged the boy's hockey aspirations by building an ice rink in the backyard of the Maslak residence. "We used to love watching the kids play hockey," Maslak later recalled. "We had a big window in the kitchen and my mother and father – Terry's grandparents – I would watch them for hours and hours. In fact, my dad and I strung chicken wire across the window so the pucks wouldn't break it."[1]

In the winter, the Sawchuk brothers also played shinny on the nearby frozen rivers of Winnipeg, often using a piece of frozen horse dung for a puck and newspapers to protect their legs. Terry's favorite goalie was Montreal Canadiens star George Hainsworth, and in the late 1930s the young boy often listened to the Habs games on radio. During this time Mitch Sawchuk became an accomplished goalie in the Winnipeg Recreational League. Terry followed in his footsteps, and already excelled in such sports as baseball and football.

Mitch suddenly died at 17 from a heart ailment, devastating his young brother, who then dedicated himself to also becoming a goalie. Later that year Terry was in the nets for Hospeler of the Bantam Playgrounds League, and was at centre the following year, netting eight goals in one game and winning the scoring title. He also played local football in the summer, his rough play earning him the nickname Butch, but a severe arm and elbow injury resulted in his right arm being about two inches shorter than the left one. Sawchuk hid the debilitating injury from his domineering mother.

Over the next few years young Terry grew in height and inherited his dead brother's goalie equipment. "The pads were around the house," he once recalled, "and I fell into them."[2] In 1942 he was recruited to play for the Esquire Red Wings, a local Midget boy's team managed by Bob Kinnear, the western scout for the NHL's Detroit Red Wings. "Terry was about eleven or twelve, husky and chubby. He was a defenseman with his school team," Kinnear remembered. "He was one of a hundred or so kids who hung around my outdoor rink. We always needed equipment and I recall him saying he had a pair of pads at home so I told him to bring them down."[3]

The Wings scout saw great potential in the young netminder, who was soon the best Midget prospect in the Winnipeg area. Kinnear was very impressed by the boy's peculiar crouch-style, in which he relied on his low centre of gravity to make quick reflex leg saves and remain low on rebounds and screen shots. Taking his goaltending duties very seriously, young Terry refused to go to movies because he thought the glare from the screen might harm his eyesight; he often avoided reading school books for the same reason. He found time to work part-time in the foundry of a farm-implement company, however, and even for a sheet-metal company.

In the fall of 1944, when Sawchuk was just 14, Kinnear arranged for him to travel to Detroit for a workout, where his revolutionary style visibly impressed the coach, Jack Adams, and the players. Returning to Winnipeg, he dislocated his elbow skateboarding, almost losing his arm to a subsequent infection, but still managed to play juvenile hockey that season. Terry moved up to the Junior Winnipeg Rangers in 1945-46, where he attracted the attention of scouts from the Chicago Black Hawks and Montreal Maroons. Louis Sawchuk wanted his son to keep his options open, but Kinnear finally convinced the family to have Terry sign a contract with Detroit.

In 1946 the Red Wings sent the young goalie, then 16, to the Galt Jr. Red Wings, their junior affiliate in the Ontario Hockey League. The next year he was moved to the Windsor Spitfires, the Wings' new junior entry, where he played four spectacular games, convincing Adams to sign the prodigy to a pro contract, with a $2,000 signing bonus. Adams shipped young Terry to Detroit's second-tier farm club, the Omaha Aksarben Knights of the United States Hockey League, where it was hoped he would replace the team's regular goalie Harvey Jessiman, who disappointed in the nets.

Allowing a goal just 40 seconds into his first game with the 1947-48 Knights, Sawchuk rebounded to backstop Omaha to a 5-1 win over the Dallas Texans. Former Red Wing Mud Bruneteau, the Knights coach, tutored the young goalie, showing him how to come out of the net and cut down angles. Terry suffered a severe eye injury against Houston on December 28th, his 18th birthday, and later on watched the operation through a bevy of mirrors, as doctors temporarily extracted his eyeball, putting three stitches into it.

He returned soon after to lead the club into the playoffs, posting four shutouts and the league's lowest goals-against average to earn top rookie honours. Omaha eventually lost, but a healthy and heavier Terry happily returned home to Winnipeg, where he played baseball in the summer. Joining the Elmwood Giants, his .376 hitting average led the Mandak League, receiving interest from such Major League Baseball teams as the Cleveland Indians, Pittsburgh Pirates and St. Louis Cardinals. Sawchuk had a strong training camp in 1948, earning a promotion to the Indianapolis Capitals of the American Hockey League, where the coach, Ott Heller, instructed him on the importance of staying on his skates and not dropping to the ice, further perfecting his famous crouch. Terry shook off another serious eye ailment to lead the Capitals into the second round of the playoffs. He also earned the Dudley Red Garrett Memorial Trophy as rookie of the year. "I honestly believed even then... he was already the best goalie anyone had ever seen," recalled Ben Woit, his roommate and another future Red Wing. "Even the goals that got by him never hit the back of the net. They just trickled over the goal line after he got a good piece of them. He always got a piece of the puck."[4]

Despite another impressive training camp, Sawchuk started the 1949-50 season in Indianapolis. Summoned to the Red Wings when regular goalie Harry Lumley was injured, Terry lost his first game to Boston but then allowed only 12 goals in the next six outings. He went back to the AHL when Lumley returned, where he again led the Caps into the playoffs and was selected to the First All-Star team. Indianapolis swept past both the St. Louis Flyers and Providence Reds and into the Calder Cup finals, where the opponent was the Cleveland Barons. Terry outplayed his future goaltending partner, Johnny Bower, and Indianapolis beat the Barons in four straight to capture the Cup. The Caps' remarkable 1950 playoff run was the first time in AHL history that a team went undefeated in its march to victory.

ROOKIE OF THE YEAR

Like its AHL affiliate, the Red Wings also enjoyed great success in the spring of 1950, as Lumley backstopped them to the Stanley Cup. Adams believed that young Sawchuk was ready for the big leagues, however, and traded his starting goalkeeper to Chicago in July. Terry was in the nets for the annual pre-season game between the Cup Champs and an NHL all-star squad. Held at Olympia Stadium in Detroit, the Red Wings posted a resounding 7-1 victory. The young netminder then stunned the hockey world by posting a measly 1.67 goals-against average in his first 15 regular season games, by far the league's lowest.

The 1950-51 Red Wings were the NHL's premier team, led by established stars Gordie Howe, Ted Lindsay and Red Kelly. Detroit was far ahead of the other teams by mid-season, and Sawchuk and another rookie, Al Rollins, were involved in a tough battle for the Vezina Trophy, awarded to the goalie with the lowest goals-against average in the regular season. Adams tried unsuccessfully to have his rookie goalie abandon his unorthodox crouch style, and adopt a more traditional stance in the nets, but he eventually relented. "I am more able to move much more quickly from the crouch position," Sawchuk noted at the time. "I have better balance to move out both legs, especially when I have to kick out my leg to stop a shot. I get low because I can follow the puck better looking through the legs than I can trying to peek over shoulders and around those big bucks. It's an easier way to get hurt, I guess, but nothing has happened so far."[5]

In his leisure time the rookie could be found fraternizing with his teammates in various bars and pubs. "Terry, to my way of thinking, never had a problem drinking in the early years," former Wing Jim Peters recollected. "Heck, we were all beer drinkers. Besides, it was my experience that all goalies drank. The pressure gets to them. All the great ones like their beer - Terry, Lumley, Broda, Durnan - they all did."[6] His on-ice play seemed unaffected, as he led the Wings to a first-place finish, earning a First All-Star team selection and easily capturing the Calder Trophy as top rookie. His win marked the first, and only, time that any person in any sport was named the top rookie in three professional leagues.

Despite playing 30 less games, Al Rollins narrowly beat out Sawchuk to win the Vezina and its accompanying $1,000 cash prize. Detroit President James B. Norris matched that amount in a surprise bonus to his rookie netminder. It lessened somewhat Terry's disappointment at losing to Montreal in the first playoff round. Sawchuk then underwent elbow surgery in the summer, removing bone chips from his ailing right arm.

DYNASTY IN DETROIT

Sawchuk firmly established himself as the game's premier goalie in 1951-52, but not before showing up to training camp at 215 pounds, jovial but overweight. Horrified, Adams put him on a strict diet and training regimen. "The Uke in those early years was big in the ass and hips. When he put weight on, that's where it went," explained Lefty Wilson, the Red Wings' long-time trainer. "One of the stupidest things Adams did was bug Terry about his weight."[7] The goalie eventually lost 20 to 25 pounds, making him noticeably quicker, but the once carefree and laid-back goalie grew depressed, often appearing sullen and withdrawn to family and friends.

In spite of his changed personality, Sawchuk led the resurgent Wings to the top of the NHL mid-season. Rangers General Manager Frank Boucher claimed that the young goalie was the best he had ever seen. "I know the real test of greatness is achievement over a longer period of years and Sawchuk is just a kid, but what a kid!", he exclaimed. "He has introduced a new technique with that low crouch of his, and you'll see lots of youngsters copying that style now."[8] Terry recorded 12 shutouts, was selected to the First All-Star team and captured his first Vezina Trophy. The Red Wings finished first overall, and entered the playoffs determined to win the Cup.

Sawchuk's 1952 post-season performance remains unmatched by any goalie in NHL history. He recorded a couple of shutouts and allowed just three goals as the Wings swept Toronto in four straight, advancing to the Cup finals against the high-flying Canadiens. Montreal coach Dick Irvin boldly predicted that the Red Wings' netminding would prove to be the team's weak link, but he was dead wrong. Terry blanked the Habs three times enroute to another sweep, handing Detroit its second Cup in three years. Sawchuk posted 4 shutouts and allowed a paltry five goals in just eight games. "Didn't Irvin say Sawchuk wouldn't stand up to the pressure?", Ted Lindsay asked. "I wonder what he thinks of him now."[9] Canadiens star Maurice Rocket Richard claimed that the goalie was their club. "Another guy in the nets," he said, "and we'd have beat them."[10]

More bone chips were removed from Terry's bum elbow in another off-season surgery. He showed up at training camp gaunt and severely thin, prompting a concerned Adams to run tests on him. No physical problems were found, but the introverted, moody goalie had trouble working in a new catching mitt and started the year slowly. Losing to the Canadiens 9-0 early in season, he was then injured and temporarily replaced in the nets by young Glenn Hall. Sawchuk regained his form when he returned, leading the Wings to their fifth straight league title and earning the Vezina Trophy, as well as another First All-Star team selection. In the post-season Terry was inconsistent and allowed soft goals, and in the first round Detroit was upset by the Bruins.

"Terry took that Boston loss on himself," recalled former teammate Marcel Pronovost. "Very much so, and so did Howe. They both sat in the dressing room for a long time afterwards."[11]

For the third straight summer Sawchuk had elbow surgery. Still worried about his goalie's health, Adams arranged for further tests, but they revealed only a low blood count. With young Hall waiting on the sidelines, Terry worried constantly about being traded. His spirits were lifted when he married Patricia Ann Morey Bowman, a Detroit native whose home cooking helped him keep on the weight. Arriving at training camp heavier and healthier, Sawchuk had extra motivation when Adams bluntly announced that the position of starting goaltender was officially up for grabs. "If Sawchuk continues like this, of course he'll be our goalie," said Adams, impressed with Terry's pre-season play, "but I wouldn't hesitate to send him down to a farm team if Hall does better."[12] After a slow start, Sawchuk found his form and finished the season strongly, as runner-up to Toronto's Harry Lumley for the Vezina.

Sensational in the nets during the post-season, Terry led Detroit past Toronto, then soundly defeated the Canadiens to capture their third Cup in five years. Driving home from a golf course in the summer, he crashed his car into a tree, and had to have surgery to treat his damaged chest. It was the fifth straight off-season that the oft-injured netminder landed in the hospital. "I wish there were no summers," he sighed. "The only summer I seem to see is when I'm looking out a hospital window."[13]

Red Wings coach Tommy Ivan left for Chicago during the off-season, and was replaced by Jimmy Skinner. Detroit's playing roster remained unchanged from the previous year, but the team struggled early in 1954-55, as the talented Canadiens became the club to beat. In August Pat Sawchuk had given birth to the couple's first child, Gerald, but there were problems at home. "That (season) was a very bad year. He often came home drunk after a game or practice, and being a young, naive Catholic girl, I thought, if we have a child, and with love and nurturing, he'll change," she later recalled. "But Terry got mixed up drinking with the Detroit Lions football players; I didn't know it at the time but they drank until they threw up and then they drank some more."[14]

After an ugly 8-4 loss to the Bruins in February, Adams benched Sawchuk in favour of Glenn Hall. Rumors circulated that Sawchuk was about to retire or be traded, and that several teammates were fed up with his cavalier attitude at practice. There remains the possibility that at the time he was suffering from alcoholic hepatitis or mononucleosis. Sawchuk returned to form within time, capturing his third Vezina and rallying Detroit to its seventh straight league title. Once again the Red Wings swept the Maple Leafs in the opening play-off round and defeated the Canadiens in the finals, with a brilliant Sawchuk soundly outplaying young Habs goalie Jacques Plante. Detroit had won its second straight Stanley Cup, and fourth in six years, but the championship dynasty would not last. By the end of the summer Sawchuk had been traded, and the Red Wings would not win another Cup until 1997.

TRADED TO THE BRUINS

In the spring of 1955 Pat Sawchuk suffered a miscarriage. That summer her husband's drinking habits and abusive behavior further put a strain on the couple's embattled marriage. The goalie became emotionally distraught in June, when Adams made a blockbuster deal, trading him to Boston in a nine-player swap. Adams felt that Glenn Hall was ready for the NHL, and decided to rid himself of Terry's temperament and his $16,000-a-year salary, then tops among NHL goalies. Sawchuk felt betrayed. "I think it was the darkest day in Terry's life," Pat claimed. "He cried and cried. I mean, the guys were all so close and then to hear about it on the radio…it just ripped him apart. He gave everything to that organization and he felt like a piece of meat afterwards."[15] Good friend Marcel Pronovost was also angry. "He (Adams) traded away homegrown players who had Red Wings tattooed on their butts," Pronovost once said. "In return, he got players who weren't that dedicated to the organization."[16]

The Bruins were very happy to acquire Sawchuk, even if it was a pleasant surprise. "Oh we'd been negotiating a trade with Detroit over several players, all right, and they knew we wanted a goalkeeper," Boston General Manager Lynn Patrick later recalled. "But no goaler's name had been mentioned, and we thought it would be Glenn Hall. In our wildest dreams we didn't think we could pry Sawchuk loose. When we learned that the mysterious goaltender of our negotiations was Terry we were dumbfounded."[17]

Sawchuk faced his former Red Wing teammates during the pre-season all-star game, an annual event between the defending Stanley Cup champions and a team composed of other NHL stars. His steady goaltending failed to elevate the sad-sack Bruins, a weak team which started out strongly but eventually slipped into its customary position at the bottom of the standings. Terry recorded nine shutouts, but Boston failed to make the playoffs.

In 1956-57 Sawchuk was often spectacular in net for the Bruins, who were badly outshot almost every game. Although the embattled goalie's stellar play had the team in first place by December, he was clearly fatigued. "I lost 20 pounds in two weeks," he later said, recalling his ordeals in Boston. "I was tired all the time and sometimes in the third period I wondered if I'd be able to finish the game."[18] He eventually landed in the hospital, diagnosed with mononucleosis.

Pressed by Bruins' management to return quickly, he was back in the nets less than two weeks later, and abruptly quit after a string of sub-par games. The local public and press empathized with the exhausted goalie when coach Milt Schmidt suspended him and called up rookie Don Simmons to finish the season. Simmons played strongly in the post season, even leading Boston to a first round upset of the Red Wings. Having spent his idle time selling cars and pitching life insurance, the suspended Sawchuk soon found himself back in Detroit.

RETURN TO THE MOTOR CITY

In Detroit, Adams was disenchanted with Glenn Hall's goaltending and Ted Lindsay's efforts to form a player's union. He dealt both players to Chicago after re-acquiring Sawchuk from the Bruins, in exchange for rookie Johnny Bucyk. "I must say I was startled when I heard that Jack Adams was interested in getting him back," recalled Lynn Patrick. "We were satisfied with Don Simmons...Terry just wasn't happy in Boston. When he'd see Jimmy Skinner he'd call to him, 'When are you going to get me back?' I found he constantly needed assurance that he was great."[19]

Delighted to be back in Motown, Sawchuk soon realized that the 1957-58 Red Wings were a shadow of the former dynasty, with much of the able supporting cast having been traded away. Detroit made the playoffs, but was quickly swept by a clearly superior Montreal squad. The Red Wings finished last overall the following season, still managing to place four players on the league's Second All-Star team, including Sawchuk. By then one of the team's veterans, Terry continued to get injured often. "I remember one game against Toronto...he put his hand...down on the puck and a guy...skated right over it. Cut all the tendons," recalled former teammate Doug Barkley. "There was blood everywhere. I grabbed his arm and helped lead him to the bench. I could actually see the white of the tendons through the gash in his hand."[20]

Sawchuk was hospitalized twice in 1959-60, for severe leg cramps brought on by his heavy drinking. Diagnosed with viral neuritis, a painful inflammation of the nerves, he did not return until February. The battle-weary goalie helped the Wings make the playoffs, but they quickly lost to the more talented Maple Leafs.

The following season, concerned about Terry's fragile health, Detroit adopted a two-goalie system, calling up Western Hockey League star Hank Bassen. Bassen carried the load. 'Terry could not stand to be second fiddle," Pronovost recalled. "He couldn't stand not playing at this point in his career and he went upstairs to management and asked to be traded."[21]

Sawchuk felt better when later he received more playing time, arid coach Sid Abel's hunch to start him in the playoffs paid off, with the veteran backstopping the Wings to the finals against Chicago. A shoulder injury sidelined him, however, and Bassen could not stop the Hawks from claiming the Cup. Terry again contemplated retirement that summer. 'There were only two things which rocked Terry's life and career. The first was being traded by Jack Adams to Boston in 1955, and the second was the two goalie system," Pat Sawchuk later said. "He hated sharing his net. In time, he adjusted to it, but at first he considered it a personal slap in the face! He sometimes mumbled about quitting, but he couldn't. It was his life. It was the only thing he knew how to do."[22]

Bassen and Sawchuk shared duties again in 1961-62, but the dismal Wings finished in fifth place, out of the playoffs. Sawchuk's bloated goals-against-average of 3.33 was a career worst, and in the off-season he attempted to revive his career by toiling with Lefty Wilson to develop a goalie mask, following the lead of innovator Jacques Plante. Prior to the start of the new season, Abel announced that the team would carry only one goalie on the roster, and the ensuing three-way battle between Sawchuk, Bassen and newcomer Dennis Riggin compelled the vet to look for any edge he could get. With a large family to feed and losses mounting in his failed off-ice business ventures, Terry was not ready to give up his pro hockey paycheques.[23]

Terry was also motivated to don a mask by the dire need to protect his face. "As a physician I always found it amazing that these goaltenders of that era could do what they did – especially Terry, because his deep crouch put his face much closer and in line with the path of the puck," Wing physician Dr. Wapatono recalled. "I sutured Terry's face countless times. I remember one time, the lower section of his nose had separated from his face. We stitched it back and he returned to the game."[24] His wife claimed that he fought the mask at first, but slowly got used to it. "It got that it gave him renewed confidence", she noted, "and he'd dive for shots that he would never have before."[25]

Terry felt rejuvenated and quickly won back the starting position; unbeaten in the first ten games, he was a candidate for MVP honors by mid-season. "I don't care how long you play this game, you still flinch when someone lets one go at your head," he claimed. "Now that I've tried a mask, I can't figure out why anyone plays without one."[26] Sawchuk suffered a severe hand injury, however, and the Wings barely made the playoffs. Detroit advanced to the finals by beating the Hawks in a high scoring series which featured eight goals by Chicago's Bobby Hull, but the more talented Leafs prevailed against Terry's stellar play to take the Cup.

In 1963-64 the battle-weary veteran accepted a back-up role to the young, acrobatic rookie, Roger Crozier; providing solid netminding when called upon. Sawchuk also recorded his 95th shutout, a 1-0 blanking of the Canadiens, to break George Hainsworth's NHL record. By the new year, Crozier was back in the minors and the veteran was leading his resurgent team into the playoffs. Once again, Terry and the Wings prevailed over Chicago only to fall to the superior Leafs in the finals. After the season, Detroit sportswriters voted the goalie as team MVP.

DRAFTED BY TORONTO

Detroit left Terry unprotected in the annual waiver draft, and Toronto picked him up. "Sawchuk will help us. With Terry and Johnny Bower rotating in the nets, we'll be tough to beat," boasted Leaf GM Punch Imlach. "I tell my players to tear up their birth certificates and I'll tell Terry the same thing. Good old guys like Kelly, Bathgate, Horton, Bower and Sawchuk don't deteriorate as fast as ham-and-eggers. Being former all-stars they can come down a long way and still be better than most."[27]

The veteran relished another shot at the championship with the powerhouse Leafs; after beating out contenders Don Simmons and Gerry Cheevers for the back-up spot, he allowed eleven goals in his first nine games. "Most goalies start out as loners. But Terry never changed," Bower noted. "More and more the group on the team left him alone. Nobody wanted to risk saying anything that might upset him."[28] The veteran netminding duo captured the Vezina Trophy, but the third-place Leafs bowed to Montreal in the playoffs.

Terry and Pat tried hard to repair their family life in the off-season; Pat and the six children had visited Toronto at Christmas but she suspected he had been unfaithful. In June, Sawchuk had a back operation after injuring it playing golf, and worked hard at rehabilitation. Before the season started, he went home to comfort his father Louis, in mourning after the sudden death of Anne Sawchuk, Terry's mother, from a brain aneurysm.

Imlach protected both veterans in the waiver draft, but in 1965-66 Bower and Sawchuk were a study in contrasts. Whereas the steady Bower practiced energetically, the consistent and oft-injured Sawchuk was lackadaisical. "I figure I only have so many saves left in me," he earnestly explained. "I want to save them all for the games."[29] His bad back prevented him from fully crouching, leaving him upright and vulnerable. The Leafs barely made the playoffs and Sawchuk, replacing a flu ridden Bower, was no match for the powerful Canadiens, who swept past Toronto in four games.

THE GLORY OF 1967

Terry endured off-season back surgery again, and had to be talked out of retirement by Imlach. His early play was surprisingly strong, and kept Bower on the bench. "Our goaltending is the reason we're in first place," Imlach noted in November. "Sawchuk has been fantastic! I think he's playing the best hockey in his career right now. He's even better than when he was playing with Detroit in the fifties."[30] The Leafs stumbled, however, when both goalies went down with injuries. Terry came back in February to post his the career shutout, a 3-0 blanking of the Hawks. "I don't know what to say, I wasn't expecting this," he quipped to reporters after the game. "The first hundred are the hardest."[31] The Leafs finished third with a late surge, still far behind first place Chicago.

Toronto faced the Black Hawks in the opening round of the playoffs, but the veteran team was the underdog against Chicago, an offensive powerhouse which had generated an NHL-record 264 regular season goals. Sawchuk backstopped the Leafs to a 2-1 series lead, but in game four Chicago's snipers chased the battle-weary goalie from the nets in a 4-3 win. Coach Imlach opted to start Bower for the pivotal fifth game, but he was injured in the first period; Terry was in the net after the intermission, the Hawks leading 2-1.

Led by Stan Mikita and Bobby Hull, whose curved sticks were renowned for unleashing lethally hard shots, Chicago immediately stormed the Maple Leafs' zone. Sawchuk turned back many great scoring chances but late in the period Hull broke in and blasted one of his 100-mph slapshots at the net. The bullet caught Terry flush in his bad left shoulder, glancing off his forehead and flying into the crowd. Terry slumped to the ice like he was shot, lying there motionless and obviously injured. The crowd grew silent, thinking the shot might have killed him. Having lived with the fear that his shot might kill someone someday, Hull nervously watched along with other players as trainer Bob Haggert rushed to the fallen goalie's side, asking him if he was okay. "I stopped the fucking shot, didn't I," he groggily replied. "Now help me up, and I'll stone those sons of bitches!"[32] He had turned away 36 shots by the game's end, a 4-2 Leafs win. "It woke me up, I guess," he conceded afterwards. "I was scared shitless every time they got near me."[33] Toronto won game six, advancing to the Cup finals.

"The way Terry stood up and challenged Hull and Mikita in that series, it was truly amazing to witness," says Ron Ellis, a right wing on that Leafs team. "He wore these battered old shoulder pads, the same ones he'd used since junior, and they were in tatters. And his chest protector was nothing more than a piece of felt. But he'd charge out there, absolutely fearless, and just keep putting his body in the way of those shots. I can only imagine the pain he must have endured. When that series was over, Terry's entire upper body was just black and blue. I've never seen anything like it. And I've never seen anyone display as much courage under fire."[34]

Well rested, Bower replaced the clearly tired Sawchuk early in the finals, backstopping Toronto to a 2-1 series lead. Certain that his capable partner would carry the load the rest of the way, Terry showed up just before the start of the next game, nursing a serious hangover from a drinking binge the previous night. Bower was injured again, this time during the warm-ups, and the shaky Sawchuk took to the nets. The Canadiens blasted six pucks past him, and the series was tied. Terry found an inner reserve of strength for the fifth game, leading the Leafs to a 6-2 win, and was nothing short of sensational in the deciding contest. Stopping point-blank shots by Jean Beliveau and Henri Richard, he blanked the Habs 3-0 to lead Toronto to its fourth and final Stanley Cup of the 1960s.

"I'm too tired to dance around," Sawchuk sighed during the post-game celebrations in the dressing room, "and I don't like champagne." Hinting at retirement, he then noted that the 1967 Cup victory was his crowning moment in hockey. "I'm not saying this is my last game," he claimed, "but I'm going to give it a lot of thought in the next few weeks."[35] Weeks later, the veteran netminder was selected at the team's Most Valuable Player for the 1966-67 season. "I've got a picture of Sawchuk taken from the 1967 Playoffs, The guy looked like he was 104 years old.", former Leaf forward Brian Conacher later recalled. "Terry had an awful lot of hard miles on him by that stage of his career and he'd had a phenomenally tough series. He was bruised and beaten up from head to toe - and obviously he was completely exhausted."[36]

THE KING IN LOS ANGELES

The Maple Leafs 1967 Stanley Cup victory marked the final chapter in the era of Original Six Hockey. That summer the six-team NHL formally doubled in size. An Expansion Draft in June allowed the six new teams to build their rosters by selecting from a list of players left unprotected on waivers. Having won the lottery draft among the newcomers, the Los Angeles Kings used their first pick to select Sawchuk, unprotected by the Leafs. Kings' owner Jack Kent Cooke, a transplanted Canadian, believed that the veteran netminder could lead his first-year club to the Cup finals. Coach and Manager Red Kelly, the former Leafs star who retired to join the Kings' franchise, was somewhat more realistic. He was banking on Terry to play 30 or 40 games, help Los Angeles make the playoffs and tutor young goalie Wayne Rutledge.

Pat Sawchuk gave birth to the couple's seventh and last child that summer, and Terry wanted to focus on his family life. Unsure he wanted to play but in need of money, he eventually signed a three-year deal worth $40,000 annually, more than double his previous salary. But he was sullen and withdrawn. "He sure gave you the cold shoulder," Rutledge recalled. "He was established, not trying all that hard at camp, and we were all hustling like the dickens. If he was at a bar, say, after practice, and on of us other goalies came in, he would get up and leave, go drink someplace else."[37]

Terry eventually warmed to Rutledge, who became the go-to guy, as the oft-injured veteran seldom played. Part of Terry's problem was that he donned the very same now outdated chest protector and shoulder pads he used in the 1950s, and his refusal to try new, more protective equipment often left him battered and bruised. "As a physical specimen, he was a disaster," former Kings' Dan Woods recalled. "His shoulder looked like it had been broken and never set right. His bad arm was three or four inches shorter than the other. He'd walk all stooped over, hobbling in and out of the rink."[38]

When Terry did play, he was nowhere near his former self. "He was the greatest goalie ever, but now he has no speed left and his reflexes are shot, and anyone observing him realistically could see how vulnerable he was," observed Bill Libby in The Hockey News. "He got by only as long as the Kings threw a blanket of protection around him. When the Kings' defensemen fell apart, he was a sitting duck."[39] The entire Sawchuk clan had moved to Los Angeles together, but Terry's drinking and womanizing worsened. He also allegedly started to hit the children at times. Pat hoped that the move to California would result in a much better home life, but the closeness of his wife and children only made Terry's anger and self-doubts resurface. During a drunken, violent tantrum late in the season, he actually threw Pat out of the house on a cold winter night, further alienating himself from her and the children.

Rutledge's solid netminding helped the Kings finish second in the Western Division. Los Angeles then met the Minnesota North Stars in the opening playoff round. Kelly decided to start Terry in net, but his inconsistent play prompted the coach to switch to the more reliable Rutledge for most of the series, and his strong play forced a game seven in Los Angeles. Kelly then made the fatal mistake of starting his faltering veteran. "Wayne is a good guy, but he was no Terry Sawchuk," Kelly later explained. "I had to go with Ukey...I figured he'd come up big."[40] The North Stars pumped nine goals past the overmatched Sawchuk to coast to an easy win and the series, and disgruntled Coliseum fans peppered him with paper, programs, and pop cans. "I was never so disappointed in Terry as I was that night," Kelly later conceded. "I felt he let me down and the team down. The loss wasn't all his fault but it was the big game and he missed it, really."[41]

THIRD TIME A RED WING

Having predictably soured on his veteran keeper, Jack Kent Cooke dealt him to the Red Wings prior to 1968-69 for Jimmy Peters Jr., whose father was a former Wing teammate of Terry's in the 1950s. "I'm happy to be coming back to Detroit," he related. "You know there are only two places I really wanted to play and Detroit is number one if I had to leave Los Angeles."[42] The Wings wanted him to be a calming influence on regulars Roy Edwards and Roger Crozier, particularly the emotional, high-strung Crozier. "For the first time in his career, the pressure was off Terry. I think he liked the role of back-up," former teammate Alex Delvecchio claimed. "He was near the end of his career and had accepted his destiny...he liked the salary and now he didn't have to work hard for it. I found him almost happy in that last year in Detroit."[43]

Pat Sawchuk, however, recalled that family life continued to suffer back in Motown. Years of emotional and physical abuse, fuelled by Terry's heavy drinking, had taken their toll, and the goalie was more withdrawn than ever from family, friends and fans. "I would sit down and sign all these things for him," she claimed, "I hate to say it, but a lot of Terry Sawchuk's autographed pictures were his wife's signature. But that's what Terry got to be like."[44] When Pat filed for divorce, Sawchuk's moods became even darker. He appeared in just 13 games, and the Wings missed the playoffs.

THE BIG APPLE

New York Rangers' GM and Coach Emile Francis had tried to acquire Terry as a back-up to young Ed Giacomin in the mid-1960s, and eagerly dealt Larry Jeffrey and Sandy Snow to get him in June. "All we want from Terry is 12 or 15 games," Francis asserted, "just enough to give Ed Giacomin an occasional rest."[45] The veteran showed up at camp enthusiastic and ready to practice hard. The powerful Rangers were in first place for most of 1969-70, and Sawchuk was elated to be part of a winning atmosphere.

The move to New York had once again distanced him from his family. He reluctantly accepted Pat's request for divorce, which was made on the grounds of extreme and repeated cruelty. Sawchuk stopped his child-support payments, and in desperation she discreetly sorted out her financial problems with Rangers management, which was sympathetic to her struggles.

The highlight of Terry's season was a 6-0 victory over the Pittsburgh Penguins at Madison Square Gardens; it was his 103th regular season shutout. "Any night of a Sawchuk shutout was magical," Francis whimsically recalled. "Terry played well that night, and I told him so."[46] Playing only 8 games that year, the greatest goalie ever was no longer the confident star of year's past. "You don't want my autograph," he told a young fan at practice one day. "I'm all washed up."[47]

The Rangers finished in fourth place, and squared off in the post-season against the mighty Bruins. Boston's snipers chased a shaken Giacomin from the nets in the first game, an 8-2 romp. Sawchuk started game 2 but was erratic in a 5-3 defeat, and Giacomin then backstopped New York to two wins at home to tie the series. In the pivotal fifth game at Boston Gardens, held on April 14, 1970, the Bruins led late in the game 3-2 when Francis employed a delaying tactic. He replaced Giacomin with his veteran goalie. A little over a minute later, Giacomin was back in the nets; it was Terry Sawchuk's final NHL appearance. Boston held on to win, and closed out the series back in New York.

Terry returned to Detroit soon afterwards to visit his 71-year old father, in the hospital recovering from a near-fatal car accident. He then enjoyed a pleasant family dinner with Pat and the children, during which there was even talk of reconciling, as well as a family trip to Florida later that summer. He returned to New York on April 29th, eager to pack up his belongings for the return trip home, to Detroit.

THE SCUFFLE

Back in New York, Sawchuk returned to the Long Island home he rented with his Rangers' teammate, the late Ron Stewart, an old friend and roommate from their playing days together in Toronto. The two men had much in common - they were both divorced, in the twilights of their hockey careers, and infamous for losing their tempers while drinking.

After checking in at the house, Terry dined at the home of friend Ben Weiner. Then the two men headed over to E & J's Pub, a nearby sports bar frequented by Rangers' players. He met up with Stewart, seated at a table, nursing a drink. The conversation soon turned to the rented home, and Stewart reminded the goalie of the need to clean it up before returning it to the owner. Not in the mood to discuss such matters, Sawchuk shrugged him off, but Stewart persisted, reminding him of money owed for unpaid house bills. Sawchuk angrily pulled out a wad of money and threw $190 at his roommate, and told him to get lost. They were soon pushing and shoving each other inside the bar. Terry swung at Stewart but missed, allegedly hitting a man seated nearby. A pub bartender then intervened, sending the two men outside.

The two Rangers continued to wrestle outside, and Weiner pulled Terry off his teammate. Stewart drove off in his car, and Weiner and Sawchuk returned to the pub, the latter still noticeably angry. "I'm going to bed," he announced soon after, "but before I do I'm going to find that bastard"[48] Sawchuk sped off in his car towards home, and a concerned Weiner followed in his own automobile.

Sawchuk and Stewart continued their argument on the front lawn of the Long Island home, and Stewart ordered his girlfriend, Rosemary Sasso, inside just before Weiner arrived. Weiner arrived to find the two men wrestling on the ground, and grabbed Terry's waist, pulling him away. Sawchuk then lost his balance and tumbled on top of Stewart, who was on the ground after supposedly tripping over a barbecue grill. He fell heavily upon his roomate's raised knee, and rolled to the ground in obvious pain. When Stewart realized

Terry was not faking, he had Rosemary call Rangers' team physician Dr. Dennis Nicholson. The doctor arrived and found Terry in apparent shock. "He was pale and had extremely low blood pressure," he recalled. "The shock must have been from the pain."[49] The goalie reluctantly agreed to be driven to the hospital by ambulance.

THE TRAGIC DEMISE

Initial x-rays at Long Beach Memorial Hospital showed nothing wrong, but subsequent tests revealed serious damage to Terry's gall bladder and liver. His gall bladder was removed in an operation on May first, but the liver remained severely damaged. After improving somewhat, Sawchuk complained of serious pains on May 11th, and his blood pressure dropped noticeably. Visiting Terry in the hospital, Dr. Nicholson was quite concerned about his severely weakened condition.

A second procedure on May 14th removed blood from his lacerated liver, but surgeons, unable to locate the source of the bleeding, elected to localize it by wrapping the liver in abdominal tissue: Listed in poor condition after the surgery, Sawchuk's status was upgraded to stable the next day, when he was visited by his brother, Gerald, and eldest son, Jerry. "I hardly recognized him," Jerry later admitted, recalling how he walked right past his own father at first. "He was so thin and haggard-looking."[50]

Emile Francis visited the stricken netminder soon after. "We found out when a doctor at the hospital phoned my office to tell us one of our hockey players was in the hospital and had already undergone two operations," he remembered. "I was in Quebec at the time on a scouting trip and I did not know any of my players were still in New York, let alone a hospital. I flew back to New York immediately and went to see Terry."[51] Resting in intensive care, weak and semi-conscious, Terry told his boss that he was the one throwing the punches, and that the incident was not Stewart's fault. The goalie also asked that nobody tell his dad about the mishap because he would worry too much. Louis Sawchuk was still recovering from his car crash in the hospital.

The first public news of the incident appeared in the May 22nd edition of The New York Times newspaper; it was reported that Terry was lying seriously ill in a local hospital. Stewart flatly denied to reporters any knowledge of his roommate's condition. Deciding to get a scoop on the story, freelance journalist Shirley Walton Fischler, wife of sportswriter Stan Fischler, visited the hospital the next day. Using her maiden name to disguise herself as a Rangers fan, she showed up at Terry's semi-private room with a bouquet of roses. Staring out the large window overlooking the Reynolds Channel, the sickly, lonely goaltender welcomed her company. "I can't tell you if this is a good hospital or not," he said. "I've been doped up for so long, I don't know. They still don't know if I'll recover from this. And it was so bad for awhile that I really didn't care. I'm still full of tubes and my back is bothering me from lying here so long."[52] Sawchuk claimed that the injury was a complete fluke accident; raising his thin and bony arms, he said, "Look. Look at me. I can never come back from this."[53] That fateful quote was the bi-line for Fischler's story, which The Times ran days later.

Jerry Sawchuk visited his father at the hospital a few times between May 23rd and 25th, and delivered a get well card on behalf of the family. Terry's damaged liver continued to collect blood, and on May 27th a chest x-ray revealed a build-up of fluids in the lungs. Terry experienced more severe liver pains the following morning, and was draining blood. When Francis visited the hospital, he was so concerned with his goalie's weary state and grey-colored skin that he finally convinced the doctors to have Terry moved to New York Hospital. By then Sawchuk was listed in critical condition, and the Rangers GM knew that the major Manhattan infirmary specialized in acute illnesses, and was much better equipped to deal with the veteran's fragile condition.

Francis accompanied Terry in the ambulance drive to New York the next morning. "Cat, we've been through so much together, so many good moments," the stricken player confided as he lay on the stretcher of the speeding vehicle. 'This would be a helluva way to go out. Damn it, we've come back before and we're going to make it this time, too!"[54]

Extensive tests at New York Hospital on May 30th revealed that major bruising and bleeding had left Sawchuk's liver critically damaged. He was rapidly getting worse, and the extensive internal damage necessitated immediate life-saving surgery. The Rangers' GM recalled the scenario when Terry met with the doctors:

> I was there and they told him he was in serious condition and that they'd have to operate right away. They also said he had a 50-50 chance of coming out of this, that there were no guarantees, that if things didn't go well, school's out. Terry didn't flinch. He faced the situation head on. After the doctors were done, I'll never forget the look on his face - he just looked straight ahead and said, "get me a priest."[55]

After seeing the priest, Sawchuk was wheeled into the operating room. 'When he went by me, he took a ring off his finger and gave it to me," Francis related. It was a Detroit Red Wing ring."[55] The goalie told Francis to give it to his son Jerry, and asked him to give the boy a decent shot at becoming a pro goalie.

Acute abdominal surgery was performed on Terry's lacerated liver by the surgeon-in-chief, Dr. Frank Glen, and the bleeding was stopped by securing the bleeding arterial vessels with sutures. The operation was successful, but Francis was told that the next forty-eight hours would be critical. Terry was moved to intensive care in critical but stable condition around 10 p.m.; early the next morning, around 8 a.m., he went into cardiac arrest after experiencing respiratory failure. Attempts to resuscitate him repeatedly failed, and he was pronounced dead at 9:50 a.m., May 31, 1970.

An autopsy performed that afternoon by Dr. Elliot Gross revealed that Sawchuk never really had a chance. "It was a case of his being in such bad shape when he was brought here," a hospital spokesperson asserted, "and our not being able to revive him."[56] The immediate cause of death was found to be a large blood clot to both pulmonary arteries leading to the lungs, but the discovery of smaller clots in peripheral blood vessels, and larger ones in the liver's hepatic vein and vernacular, showed that he would have inevitably died.

Francis was called down to the nearby morgue on Second Avenue to identify the body, and remembered that the attendant did not even know who Terry Sawchuk was. "A chap came out and said 'Is anyone here named Francis?' I identified myself and he told me to follow him," he recalled. "We went down a couple of flights of stairs and he opened the door and there were about thirty bodies lying there and the first thing that hit me was that they were in bags just like the bags we used to carry hockey sticks in. And there was his head out of one end of the bag with the tag around his neck. They had Terry Sawchuk written on the bag."[57]

THE ACCIDENT IS INVESTIGATED

About a week before Sawchuk's death, the Rangers decided the situation was serious enough to warrant hiring Nicholas Castellano, Long Island's top defense attorney, to represent Stewart. Pat Sawchuk and her father, Ed Morey, allegedly felt that the Rangers were covering up details of the injury, and team executives feared Stewart going to trial, as well as the negative publicity it would engender.

Just prior to his death, the press coverage and rumors surrounding Terry's original injury prompted District Attorney William Cahn to launch an investigation. Sawchuk's subsequent death sped up the legal process. An initial police probe was to determine if the case should be brought before a grand jury, which would in turn decide if manslaughter charges were to be levied against Stewart. At the time of the incident in late April police concluded the mishap to be accidental, and neglected to file a formal report. The day after his death, however, homicide detectives in Nassau County, Long Island reopened the case.

On June 8 the District Attorney subpoenaed Francis, Stewart, Ben Weiner and Rosemary Sasso to appear before a grand jury hearing. He met with the four witnesses on June 3rd for preliminary questioning, finding all of them to be very cooperative. Weiner later corroborated Sasso's assertion to The New York Post that Terry was coughing up blood well before the accident. Dr. Elliot Gross added fuel to the controversy. "There was a trauma or blunt force injury to Terry's liver, but the exact cause of death was a blood clot that travelled from a vein in a pulmonary artery," Gross claimed. "But forty year old men don't just get pulmonary embolisms."[58] What the doctor failed to mention was that this particular forty year old man lay in a hospital with a severely damaged liver for almost an entire month.

RON STEWART'S STORY

Stewart told his version of the incident to The New York Post shortly before the grand jury hearing. "All his lifetime Terry took much worse falls on the ice and he always bounced back...and then he trips on top of me and suddenly his life is ended," he said. "A fall like that, just like a thousand he's taken on that hard ice and nothing ever happened to him...It's all like a bad dream when I look back on it now."[59]

Discussing the money dispute that triggered the scuffle, Stewart claimed that Terry became enraged when the issue of unpaid bills came up.[60] He also asserted that back at the rented house an angry Sawchuk kept advancing at him. "I had backed away and tripped over a metal barbecue pit that had been lying on the lawn from the day before when it fell over," he alleged. "It was dark at the time and when Terry came after me, with Weiner still holding on, he caught his foot in my leg and fell on top of me...but I think he hit himself against one of the protrusions on the cooker - or possibly against my knee."[61]

THE WAKE

Pat Sawchuk was perplexed as to why she was not consulted on the wake for Terry organized by her brother-in-law Gerald. 'The morning of the wake was awful," she admitted. "I had to get these seven kids ready for something that they didn't know anything about. They were sad and they were scared. I've always found funerals and wakes barbaric...I mean, to drag families and young kids through something that tears them apart is awful."[62] Gerald reacted bitterly to her greeting of members of family members. "He said Terry and I were divorced, that I shouldn't have made such a display," she recalled, "that my actions kissing Terry's family didn't look right now, that the kids should come out and sit by Terry's casket, but that I should stay in the anteroom and keep myself scarce."[63]

When she retreated to the anteroom, people still lined up to offer her their sympathies. "Gerald came back in and said I'd been there long enough and that I should leave, that it didn't look right, people coming to see me," she admitted. "So I left the kids with either Rose Jollie or the Hanlons and I went out to the car. I was real upset with Gerald. Out at the car I had a good cry."[64] Nick Maslak, Terry's uncle, became infuriated when he found Pat sobbing in

47

the parking lot. "All I know, she belongs where she is and that's by her husband," Maslak bluntly informed his nephew "and she could do what she wants with him. You have no say in it!"[65]

Maslak was further angered that Gerald had arranged the chairs around Terry's casket, supposedly in case people rushed the coffin. "Who told you this? Where did you come from," Maslak said, again chastising his nephew. "I can see you never were at a funeral before. When your mother died, did they have chairs like this? Around her? You're making a mockery out of this. You're not going to have it this way."[66] As Nick removed the chairs, an embarrassed and irate Gerald stormed off.

Maslak later found Ron Stewart loitering outside the funeral home. The Ranger forward told him that he was afraid to go inside to pay his respects because his presence might create a scene. Maslak comforted Stewart, and reminded him that he had been a friend of Terry's and had every right to pay his respects. He then led Stewart inside.

Several pro hockey players attended Sawchuk's wake, including his former teammates. "All the old gang, the old Red Wings, we all went to the funeral parlour," the late Lefty Wilson recalled. "He looked so good lying there in the coffin- shit, he was only 40 years old - and I thought he could just get out of there and put the pads on, you know?"[67]

THE LAST FAREWELL

The memorial service was held on June 5, 1970, at our Our Lady of La Salette Catholic Church in Berkeley, Michigan. Among those in attendance were League President Clarence Campbell, Punch Imlach, Stewart, several of Terry's former teammates, and representatives from each of the 14 NHL teams. The mass was presided over by Father John Gordon, and Rever and E.A. Vecchio delivered an eloquent and moving sermon. After the service, Terry's casket was carried out by pallbearers Francis, Weiner, Giacomin, Pronovost and Kinnear. Michigan State Troopers then escorted over 150 cars and limousines to the burial site, at Mount Hope Cemetery in nearby Pontiac. The funeral procession passed by Pontiac General Hospital in deference to Louis Sawchuk, still under the care of doctors and unable to attend.

The late Johnny Wilson, a former Red Wing teammate, used to drive by Mount Hope Cemetery three or four times a week, on the way to work. "Old Uke's grave is right by the side of the road," he once noted. "Every time I go by I think about him and wonder how things might have turned out if he'd lived. It is funny how hockey fans seem more interested in Terry now than when he was alive."[68]

THE GRAND JURY HEARING

Francis, Stewart and Weiner flew to New York immediately after the funeral, to attend their scheduled appearances before the Grand Jury Hearing. Proceedings were held in Mineola, Long Island, and others called to testify included Rosemary Sasso, Dr. Denis Nicholson, Dr. Elliot Gross, Nassau Country police detective Conrad Kessler, and bartenders Margaret Wilson and Joe Crane, who both served drinks to Sawchuk and Stewart on the fateful day of the incident.

After hearing over three hours of testimony, the grand jury deliberated for 30 minutes before ruling that the death was accidental. District Attorney Calm noted that claims of Sawchuk coughing up blood well before the incident could not be verified, but that there was no evidence of forceful blows between Sawchuk and Stewart. A childish and senseless verbal dispute had degenerated into a scuffle, Calm told reporters afterwards, and Terry's injuries from the resulting fall caused the embolism leading to death. The District Attorney announced that Stewart was absolved from any wrongdoing, and that his office considered the case officially closed.[69]

Jerry Sawchuk, Terry's oldest child, still believes that his father's death was entirely accidental. "His hockey career was finished, and life off the ice had never been easy for him," he surmised. "It was, like, the play was over, the game had ended. It was, like, the end of his time..."[70] Jerry claimed his family never blamed Stewart for what transpired:

We know he's had to carry this around with him all his life, and nobody can put themselves in his shoes to know how much it may or may not have haunted him. Dad has the blame to shoulder and he paid for it with his life, plain and simple.[71]

LEGACY: A GOALTENDING LEGEND

Terry Sawchuk was inducted into the Detroit Red Wings' Hall of Fame on February 4, 1971, during a pre-game ceremony at a game against the Rangers, in old Olympia Stadium. Less than a month later, he was posthumously awarded the 1971 Lester Patrick Memorial Trophy for outstanding service to hockey in the United States. The customary three-year waiting period for entrance into the Hockey Hall of Fame was waived for the great goaltender, and he was inducted that same season. "I have done a lot of eulogies and a lot of presentations at the Hockey Hall of Fame and elsewhere, but Terry's induction was the most emotional and difficult to do," Emile Francis asserted, "but Terry's induction was a natural. He was in a class all his own, really. I've seen a lot of great ones, but Terry's still above the rest."[72]

A special display of Sawchuk's goalie equipment still resides in the Hall. A few years later, in 1974, hockey's greatest goaltender was also inducted to the Manitoba Hall of Fame, and selected as that province's greatest hockey player of the 20th Century.

Sawchuk's legacy was revisited in the 1990s. In 1991 a sports arena in East Kildonan, Manitoba was rechristened Terry Sawchuk Memorial Arena. The Red Wings officially retired Terry's No. 1 jersey in an emotional pre-game ceremony in 1994. Over 21,000 grateful fans and a bevy of Wing oldtimers roared with approval as a commemorative banner bearing his name and number was hoisted to the rafters. "As I look back on it now, I'm glad they didn't retire Dad's number for many years," admitted Michael Sawchuk, "because now, at the ceremony, we were all adults; some of us had our children with us on the ice. It meant much more to us because we could fully appreciate the moment."[73]

Sawchuk's legacy was again remembered during the NHL's 2000-2001 season, when his record of 447 career wins was eventually eclipsed by Patrick Roy of the Colorado Avalanche., "I want to find out about him as a man, as a goaltender, what his career was like," Roy admitted, months before. "One of the great things about this is that the closer I get to the record, there will be more and more things written and said about Terry Sawchuk. People will sort of re-discover him."[74]

In October, 2000, Jerry Sawchuk took part in the special ceremony honouring Roy's breaking of the milestone, but still felt protective of his dad's achievement. "I'd be lying if I said I wasn't a little sad about it," he admitted after meeting Roy at center ice, "but life moves on. We're just lucky to be here, to be part of this. And to see Patrick win it, it just couldn't be any better."[75]

Sawchuk and Roy are often cited as the greatest two goaltenders ever, and this inevitably leads to comparisons. "All goalies are kind of goofy, I guess, and I'm sure Patrick is a little eccentric," Doug Barkley claimed. "But, Terry? Now this guy was eccentric. He wouldn't sign autographs. Didn't let people go near him. He was a real loner."[76] The late Red Wings' coach Jimmy Skinner has scouted and watched NHL hockey for more than half a century, and once claimed that Sawchuk was the best he ever saw. "I wouldn't trade two Patrick Roys for one Terry Sawchuk," he remarked.[77] Ted Lindsay recalls that Terry's first years in the NHL were his finest. "For the first five years of his career, there has never been a better goaltender to play the game," he asserted not long ago. "And as far as I'm concerned, they can play for another thousand years and still won't find another like him."[78]

Sawchuk is remembered as a netminding innovator, the first goalie to adopt the crouch style, bending so deeply in the nets that his chin almost touched his padded knees. He developed the crouch because he had to, since his left arm was shorter than the right, the result of his childhood injury. "He had to stay down low," recalled former Red Wing Carl Liscombe, "or he couldn't completely cover that side of the net."[79] Red Kelly claims that Terry's widebody frame was the secret to his success. "He stood up. You didn't see a lot of the goal when you were coming in, trying to put the puck past him," Kelly noted. "He sure could cover the net. He never went down a lot. When he went down, he got up quickly. He always crouched low to see that puck coming through."[80] For generations, young goaltenders across the continent imitated The Sawchuk Crouch, including Hall of Famer Glenn Hall, who later developed his own peculiar butterfly style.

Bower recently said that Terry's crouch was the best he ever saw. "He remained square to the shooter as much as possible, but he cheated on rushes in that he wasn't the quickest goalie to come out and cut down the angle," said the former Leafs great "But his cat-like reflexes were what allowed him to stay a little deeper in the net."[81] Skinner recalled that Sawchuk never left his feet when he was in his crouch. "You wouldn't see him go down so quickly like the goalies today," the former Red Wings coach said. "He was always injured, but ever toward the end, when he was over the hill and playing with the Rangers, he was still outstanding. He was the best."[82]

The incredible statistics compiled by Sawchuk re-affirm his great legacy. He held the record for most regular season shutouts until it was broken in 1990 by New Jersey's Martin Brodeur; he was an NHL goalie for 21 seasons, a feat only matched by Brodeur and Gump Worsley. Early in his career with Detroit, Terry posted five straight seasons with a goals-against average below two per game, and remains the only player in any sport to capture top rookie honours in three different pro leagues.

His achievements in the NHL speak for themselves: Calder Trophy as top rookie; four Vezina Trophies; four Stanley Cups; seven All-Star team selections; and eleven All-Star games played. These feats are all the more impressive in light of his dark and ongoing battle with alcoholism, his turbulent family life, and the endless series of injuries he endured: punctured lungs, ruptured discs, a blocked intestine, a ruptured spleen, infectious mononucleosis, severed hand tendons, a broken instep, a dislocated elbow, a twice-broken nose, and over 600 stitches.

Sawchuk's various ailments made him a moodier person. "One day he would say hello to you," recalled fellow netminder Worsley, "and the next day he wouldn't bother to."[83] Skinner concurred. "He was a difficult person, no question," he agreed. "He was a miserable guy in a lot of ways. I think a lot of that was because he lived hockey 24 hours a day. He'd take the game home with him. He'd take the game to bed with him. It consumed him."[84]

"My dad was hard to get close to," admitted Terry's son, Jerry, years later. "There wasn't much there with him. It was sort of a funny thing. By the time you were growing up and had the chance to maybe get to know him at a different level, he was gone." Jerry claimed his father was a good man who cared about his family; he fondly recalled a fishing trip in northern Ontario, when a big, burly bear broke into the cabin after smelling cooked fish. "My dad grabbed me and took me to the bedroom," he remembered, "and the next thing you know he's beating the bear with a log and throwing logs at him. He took on the bear, one on one."[85]

An innovator and arguably the greatest goaltender ever, Sawchuk's unbridled love for the game of hockey should also not be forgotten. He guarded his net with persistent dedication, in an era when goalies left their heads unprotected and vulnerable, and received little protection from outdated equipment. He guarded his net in an era when most teams had little respect for the contract rights of players, particularly goaltenders, who had neither the luxury of netminding coaches nor players agents. Terry Sawchuk lasted 21 NHL seasons because he truly loved the game. "The only time Sawchuk was happy, completely, totally happy was when he was in those big, brown, bulging pads," wrote Joe Falls of The Detroit Free Press, "with his legs dangling over the trainer's table and a cigarette dangling from his lips, and he was exchanging insults with his teammates...This was the life he was born for, the life he lived for."[86]

REMEMBERING A FRIEND

Former Red Wing player Ben Woit was a teammate of Terry's, when the two started out in the minor leagues; Ben and Terry started rooming together in the late 1940s, as members of the Indianapolis Capitals. They later boarded together when they joined Detroit, and were both instrumental to those great Cup teams.

In 2014 Ben, then 86 years of age, recalled those early days. "Terry could be a really fun roomie," Ben recalled. "We used to like to go to the track to gamble on the horses and we won our fair share of races. Afterwards we would treat ourselves to a couple of beers."[87]

Woit still believes that Terry will go down as the greatest goalie ever. "To do what he did in those days, with what (little) protection he had on, those pads, no mask; it was absolutely incredible. He took a lot of stitches to the face and he was always hurt. Terry ended up paying the ultimate price, and that's partly why he should be remembered as probably the greatest goalie ever."[88]

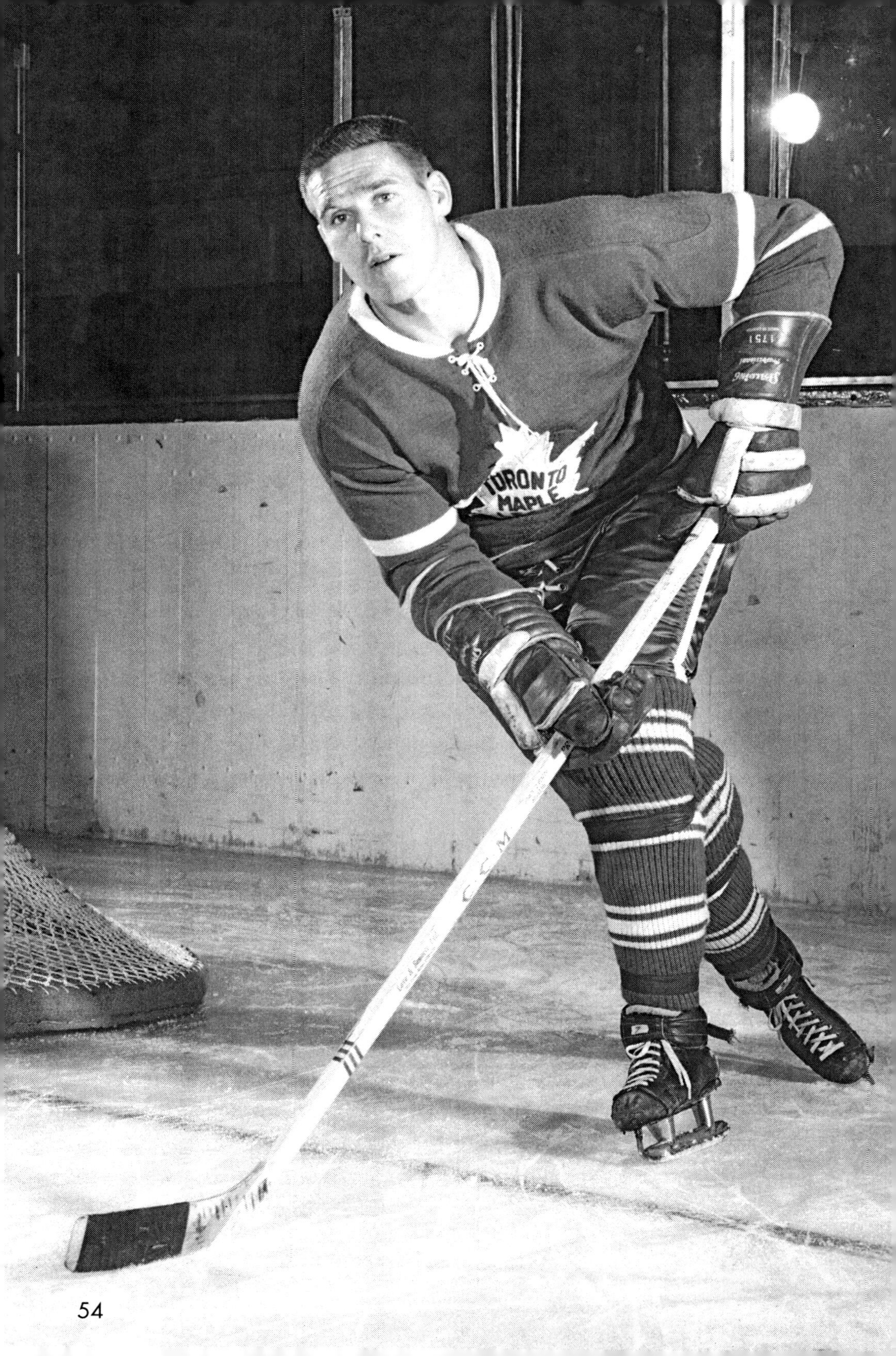
TORONTO
MAPLE
CCM

CHAPTER 3

1930 - 1974

TIM HORTON

At 44, veteran Buffalo Sabres' defenseman Tim Horton was in the twilight of a 24-year NHL career, highlighted by four Stanley Cups and seven All-Star game appearances with the Maple Leafs. In the early morning hours of February 21, 1974, Horton was driving home to Buffalo from Toronto when he crashed his European sports car on the Queen Elizabeth. He was killed instantly, his death shocking the hockey world. That night Sabres players wore black arm bands when they played at home against the Atlanta Flames, in memory of one of the greatest rearguards to play the game.

PRODUCT OF COCHRANE

Tim Miles Gilbert Horton was born January 21, 1930 at the Lady Minto Hospital in Cochrane, a community in northern Ontario. He was the oldest son of Aaron Oakley and Ethel Horton, of English and Irish descent respectively. There was not much to do for a young boy in Cochrane, a former wild frontier town which developed an economy based on the discovery of gold, silver and copper in the northern reaches. "Cochrane is as far north as you can go in Ontario without hitting James Bay," Tim's wife, the late Lori Horton, once recalled. "Oh God, it is (really) cold."[1] Like many other boys their age, Tim and his brother Gerry found solace playing ice hockey on the area's frozen lakes.

Young Tim soon developed in to one of Cochrane's most promising hockey talents. His brother Gerry once recalled that Tim scored all eight goals for his team in the last organized league game he played there. "At the end of the year they wouldn't give him the Most Valuable Player Award because he wouldn't pass the puck," Gerry claimed. "Of course, they didn't have to."[2]

Not many good jobs were available in Cochrane in the 1930s and 1940s, particularly with large employment losses in the mining sector. Like most families in the area, the Hortons were poor. Tim's parents realized that their son had few chances available to him to leave northern Ontario and find success elsewhere, but that hockey might be one way out. NHL scouts often scored the north in search of talented young players, and brought back prospects to their minor league affiliates. Concerned that their teenage son might go unnoticed playing in a remote outpost such as Cochrane, Aaron and Ethel moved the family to Sudbury. In 1945-46 young Horton played for the Copper Cliff Junior Redmen, a junior A entry in the Northern Ontario Hockey Association.

Redmen coach Jim Dewey was impressed by the 16-year-old's brute strength. At 5 foot 9 and 165 pounds, Horton was not a big kid, but he had a solid physique, his rippled arm and stomach muscles the result of countless hours of sit-ups, chin-ups and push-ups. Tim enjoyed a strong first season with the Redmen, and even showed some scoring potential with his high school team, in local Midget competitions.

The coach had originally planned to employ Horton on the right wing the following campaign, but became more impressed with the youngster's ability to keep opposing forwards away from the Redmen net. Tim became the team's premier defenseman, and perhaps its fastest skater. "He had an explosive style," recalled former Redmen teammate Sam Bettio, "and if you got in his way, he ran right over you."[3] He suffered a fractured cheekbone during the season while playing with his high school team, a condition which seemed to exacerbate his already poor eyesight. Off the ice, the near-sighted hockey player was known for wearing thick glasses.

The 1947 playoffs effectively ended for the Redmen when Horton broke his ankle, but shortly afterwards Leaf Scout Bob Wilson paid the young player a visit. Wilson was one of those NHL scouts who travelled northern Ontario in search of new hockey talent, and had become very impressed with the defenseman's play. Almost immediately he offered Tim a minor-league contract. An agreement was eventually reached between the Horton family and the Maple Leafs - Tim would continue his high school education the following season at St. Michael's College in Toronto, while playing for the school team, the St. Mike's Majors.[4] St. Michael's is a Catholic school, and there was some concern about Tim not belonging to the faith. Horton knew it was the chance of a lifetime, however, as the Majors were the famed junior club renowned as a breeding ground for future Leaf greats.

IN THE LEAFS' SYSTEM

The 1947-48 Majors were in a major re-building phase and lacked offensive power, but on defense Horton became an anchor, displaying poise and strength. Often immobilizing his opponents with his strength, his impressive puck handling skills improved as the season wore on. Tim developed a reputation for scoring late-game goals on end-to-end rushes when the forwards could not muster an attack. In spite of the team's failure to make the playoffs, Tim was voted team MVP by his teammates.

Horton became more of a leader the following year, developing into a major offensive threat from the blue line. Unquestionably the Major's best player, he was named top defenseman in OHA Junior A hockey. With his outgoing personality Tim also became more popular off the ice, and on campus he organized sight-seeing excursions to the Gardens. His familiarity with the local neighborhood reflected his own confidence that someday he would be playing there.[5]

Already impressed with his play at St. Mike's, Maple Leaf President Conn Smythe liked what he saw from Horton at the annual Maple Leaf hockey school in September 1949. Smythe wanted to add the defenseman to the Toronto Marlies to strengthen the club's bid for the Memorial Cup, but Tim did not want to face the Majors, his former team. Smythe eventually convinced him to sign a three-year contract with the Pittsburgh Hornets, a Maple Leaf affiliate in the American Hockey League. The salary, which paid Horton $4,000 a year, allowed him to buy a new sports car he wanted.

During his three seasons with the Hornets, from 1949-50 to 1951-52, Horton showed that he was destined to soon play for the Maple Leafs. With his chiseled physique and bruising style of play, he was a fan favorite. "Grim Tim (is) a kid with a rough jaw and a granite body," wrote The Toronto Telegram. "He's as hard as nails, loves nothing better than to mix it up, and is a dazzling puck manipulator."[6] Horton followed up a strong first season in Pittsburgh by leading the team to the Calder Cup Finals the year after. He evolved into an even bigger offensive threat in his final season, perfecting the art of the slap shot and scoring 12 goals. In spite of Horton's brute strength, he had relatively small, weak hands and compensated for his unimpressive wrist shot with a potent slap shot.[7] The improvement in his offense helped get him selected to the AHL's First All-Star team, and was invaluable to the Hornet's championship drive. It was also in Pittsburgh that Tim met his future wife, Dolores Lori Michalek.[8]

A STAR IN TORONTO

After the mysterious disappearance of Bill Barilko in the summer of 1951, the Maple Leafs' acute need for an offensive yet aggressive defenseman led them to Horton. His first tour of duty, a brief stay in 1952-53, was tentative. Leafs management was looking for him to be more pugnacious when he joined the club as a rookie the following year, but Tim liked to play a clean game, devoid of fighting. Coach Hap Day knew that Horton had offensive potential, but wanted him to be more of a stay-at-home rearguard. Day knew that the Leafs could not play a run-and-gun game with such offensive powerhouses as Detroit and Montreal, and thus stressed defensive play.

In spite of the 1951 Cup victory, the decade was not a very glorious one for the Maple Leafs, who struggled more often than not. In spite of the team's woes, Horton continued to develop into a strong defender. He exceeded his rookie season output of sixteen points in the first twenty-nine games of his sophomore year, 1954-55, and was eventually named to the NHL's Second All-Star Team. Tim's steady defensive play was a major reason why Toronto set a league record for fewest goals against, but there remained a large gap between the Leafs and the NHL's top teams. When Leafs scoring star Max Bentley was traded to New York, Horton replaced him on the power-play. The coach even gave Horton the number 7 jersey, previously worn by Bentley.

With renewed confidence, Horton started to bolster the weak Toronto attack by rushing the puck up the ice, just as he did for St. Mike's. On March 12, 1955, in a game against New York, Horton freewheeled past center ice, and carried the puck into the Rangers' zone. Caught with his head down, he was flattened by a heavy body check which New York rearguard Bill Gadsby threw. The hard hit fractured Horton's jaw, and then he broke his leg falling awkwardly to the ice. The injuries, which landed him in the hospital for over six weeks and ended his season, were serious enough that Horton thought he might never be able to play again."[9]

Tim underwent physical therapy after his hospital stay, and missed the first part of the 1955-56 campaign. Conn Smythe played it safe by not forcing his star player to return to action too soon. "I don't care if I have to keep Horton out of hockey for a whole season," the Maple Leaf President declared. "We're taking no chances with this guy. I never realized he was as good as he is."[10] Smythe's actual treatment of his star defenseman, however, reflected the cool attitude most NHL owners held towards their players. Tim eventually received a pay cut when he returned to action and soon after was actually fined $500 by management for indifferent play, having played cautiously at the start.[11] Logging just thirty-five games before his leg was re-set, his season ended on a sour note.

Horton's tentative play continued the following year, and the re-building Maple Leafs posted another mediocre regular season performance. Concerned about the injured rearguard's future, Maple Leafs management almost traded him to Boston during the summer, but decided to bring him back in the fall. Working hard to return from his near career-ending injuries, Tim managed a decent campaign in 1957-58. Although new coach Billy Reay did not use him as frequently, Horton still notched 26 points in 53 games, earning an invitation to the annual NHL All-Star Game.

After having struggled through much of the 1950s, the Toronto Maple Leafs hockey team embarked on a brand new era in the fall of 1958, when Punch Imlach was hired as Coach and General Manager. A no-nonsense coach who believed in discipline and hard work, Imlach was also a very good judge of hockey talent. After adding Johnny Bower, Allan Stanley and rookie Carl Brewer to the team for 1958-59, with rookie pivot Dave Keon to follow shortly after, Imlach assigned Horton to a special role. Imlach nicknamed his defenseman The General, for his ability to direct and mount an offensive attack, and made Tim an essential part of the offensive strategy. The Leafs responded to this makeover with two strong regular seasons, reaching the Cup finals in both 1958-59 and 1959-60. Imlach still had a few more players to add to the mix, but the right combination of talented youth and veteran leadership was starting to take shape. A Leafs dynasty was in the making.

THE GLORY YEARS

Having finished the disappointing 1950s on a promising note, Toronto enjoyed its greatest regular season during the Imlach era in 1960-61. With 39 wins the Leafs finished second overall to the Montreal Canadiens. In spite of Horton's stellar play on the blueline, they lost to the Detroit Red Wings in the opening playoff round.

The following year, Imlach allowed his star defenseman to develop his own game, encouraging Horton to rush the puck offensively as long as he took care of business on defense. Toronto greatly benefited from this new strategy. Tim quarterbacked the team's potent offensive attack, setting career highs with 10 goals and 38 points. Finishing second overall in the regular campaign, Toronto defeated New York and then Chicago to win the 1962 Stanley Cup. Perhaps the best player in the post-season, Horton set a new playoff record for points by a defenseman with 16 points in just 12 games.[12]

By the early 1960s, Horton was reputed to be the strongest player in a league which included Gordie Howe and Bobby Hull in their primes. Tim was not known for throwing body checks, which he felt took him out of his defensive position, but rather for immobilizing opponents. "Most opponents, even the toughest, avoided him," former NHL player Norm Ullman recalled, "because when he got close and had a chance to put those (large) arms around you, you were done. The Horton Bear Hug! It makes me shiver a little just to think about seeing a guy caught in it."[13] He earned the nickname Superman among teammates, who kidded him about his unusual strength. His bad eyesight, however, earned him other monikers such as Magoo or Cousin Weak Eyes. Horton actually warned fellow rearguard Stanley about his poor vision whenever Imlach paired them together.[14]

The Maple Leafs followed up their Stanley Cup-winning season with another strong showing in 1962-63. Toronto had become the team to beat, with Horton, Stanley, Brewer, and Bobby Baun providing the league's best defensive foursome.[15] The fearsome offensive attack was led by sniper Frank Mahovlich and skilled pivots Keon and Red Kelly, converted from defense after being acquired from the Red Wings. The Leafs finished first overall, with 82 points. Tim's offensive production dipped to 25 points, but he continued to play solid defense and was named to the NHL's Second All-Star Team. He was again perhaps the finest player on the ice during the playoffs, as the Blue shirts captured a second straight Cup.

It was during these glory years that Horton and his teammates started to drink a lot of alcohol. "They were celebrating (victory)," Lori Horton recalled, "or they were drowning their sorrows." [16] Horton and Stanley liked to party loudly at the team's hotels, often rousing their teammates out of bed. Tim was known getting physical and breaking down hotel room doors when he drank to excess.

Firmly entrenched as the team to beat by the start of 1963-64, the confident Maple Leafs got off to a fast start. Horton benefited from the positive dressing room atmosphere and had 12 points by mid-November, good numbers for a defenseman. He ended up with 29 points and was finally selected to the NHL's First All-Star Team. Tim was also runner-up to Chicago's Pierre Pilote in voting for the Norris Trophy (Best Defenseman). Toronto struggled around mid-season and finished third overall, but the talented team bested Detroit in the Cup finals to capture their third consecutive championship.

Given the club's success, Imlach was content to just let Horton play his game by that point in his career. "The story with him is that he just keeps getting better all the time, so naturally he has faith in the way he does things," Imlach admitted. "But this can be aggravating for a coach sometimes. He's going to play it the way he wants to play it. Period. There's not much you can do about it."[17]

Tim scored a career-high 12 goals in 1964-65, but the Leafs struggled to a dismal fourth-place finish and exited early from the playoffs. The string of three straight Cups ended, and matters did not get much better for the team when five players held out for better contracts prior to the start of the next training camp: Horton, Baun, Brewer, Keon and forward Bob Pulford. Although all the players eventually returned to the fold, Toronto still finished third overall, and were knocked out of the playoffs in the first round.

The 1966-67 season did not start well for the Maple Leafs. With the aging team struggling on the ice, it was often noted by hockey critics that several key players were well past their mid-30s, including goalies Terry Sawchuk and Johnny Bower, not to mention Horton, Brewer, Stanley, Kelly and captain George Armstrong. Their ages, relatively advanced for pro hockey players, earned them such nicknames as Over-the-Hill Gang and Old Folks A.C. [18]

The Maple Leafs lost ten games in a row at one point in the regular campaign before finally rebounding. Imlach became ill and was replaced behind the bench by King Clancy. "King's being doing a great job - don't get me wrong," Horton told Red Burnett of The Toronto Star, "but Punch had us straightened out before his health gave out. He proved he was a real man during that ten-game losing streak. He could have blasted us in the news media, made alot of line-up changes, and taken us apart verbally behind closed doors. He did none of those things. Instead of criticizing us he went out of his way to try to build our confidence and kept impressing us with the fact that we had too much ability to keep skidding."[19]

Toronto put together a late-season winning streak to finish third overall, and Horton was selected to the NHL's Second All-Star Team. In the opening playoff round against Montreal, the Leafs suffered numerous defensive lapses and the offensively superior Canadiens carried most of the play. Goalies Sawchuk and Bower took turns shutting down the Montreal attack, however, and the series slowly turned in Toronto's favor. The veteran Blue shirts, sensing that this might be their last chance to win a Cup together, took advantage of timely goals and persevered against the Habs.

Advancing to the 1967 Cup finals against the NHL's tap team, the powerful Black Hawks, Toronto relied on its aging defense corps to contain Chicago snipers Bobby Hull and Stan Mikita. Horton played a central role in particular, repeatedly neutralizing Hull in front of the Leaf net, and once again the veteran goalies took turns shutting down Chicago's attack. Toronto defeated the Hawks in six games, the Cup-winning goal being scored with five veteran Leafs on the ice - Horton, Stanley, Kelly, Pulford and Armstrong. [20]

END OF AN ERA

The Maple Leafs' 1967 Cup victory, their fourth of the decade, marked the beginning of the end for a great hockey dynasty. Despite of Imlach's best efforts to keep things together, the team was dismantled over the summer. Sawchuk was lost in the expansion draft to Los Angeles, one of six new NHL franchises. Kelly retired, and key players were traded, including Frank Mahovlich, Pete Stemkowski, Jim Pappin and Larry Hillman.[21]

A training camp holdout in the fall, Horton returned to have a strong season and was named to the First All-Star Team. On February 4, 1968 the defenseman also set a team record for most consecutive regular season games, 486, a streak that dated back to 1961. After having won the Cup the previous season, however, the Leafs finished fifth in the newly established Eastern Division, out of a playoff position.

Prior to the start of 1968-69, the Leafs awarded Tim the J.P. Bickell Memorial Trophy, as the team's most valuable player the previous year. Like the other original six teams, the Leafs could only protect eleven skaters, resulting in the loss of two more key players, Bobby Baun and Eddie Shack. The Leafs rebounded to finish fourth overall in the East, however, and clinched a playoff spot. With expansion having brought more scoring to the NHL, Horton was among several other veterans who posted some of their best offensive seasons ever. He notched a career-best 40 points, was selected to the First All-Star Team and was runner-up to Bobby Orr for the Norris Trophy.

The Maple Leafs club was in turmoil entering the playoffs, and Imlach's relations with several players were strained. After the Boston Bruins swept Toronto in the semi-finals, outscoring their opponent 17-0, the coach was fired and goalie Johnny Bower retired. Leaf executives Harold Ballard and Stafford Smythe were arrested for fraud soon after. Upset with Imlach's dismissal, Horton hinted at retirement and stayed away from training camp in the fall of 1969. "I was tired and the season had been long and hard," he later recalled. "For the first time, hockey was no longer fun. Also, my business partner had been after me for a long time to go full-time in our Tim Horton Donut shop business."[22]

TIM DONUT LTD.

Horton's initial business venture was not Tim Donut Ltd., the donut-shop franchising business he established in 1964 with associate Jim Charade. Tim's initial off-season interests included working at Conn Smythe's contracting company, selling classifieds for the Toronto Telegram, and opening up car dealerships with his brother Gerry.[23] A modest property company, Tim Horton Holdings Ltd., was also set up in the early 1960s, and efforts to establish a hamburger restaurant chain met with mixed results.

The first Tim Horton Do-Nut franchise opened up in Hamilton in April 1964 with little fanfare or competition. Although tea was still the beverage of choice in Canada at the time, coffee was becoming more popular in the U.S. Many steel workers living in Hamilton enjoyed coffee, as well as the large variety of fresh, hot donuts the store offered.

With the business running smoothly by 1965, Horton and Charade formed a new partnership, Tim Donut Ltd., with Tim receiving half the business in exchange for injecting capital into his associate's venture. "Dad would be out there looking for (store) locations. He also did the financing," Jeri-Lynn recalled. "I drove dad up to Sudbury and out to North Bay, looking for locations."[24] Both the Horton burger chain and donut franchise experienced cash flow problems, however, and by 1966 Hamiton businessman Ron Joyce had replaced Charade as Tim's new partner.

Joyce was an ambitious and intelligent businessman who convinced the hockey player to concentrate on developing the donut side of the business. Whereas Charade had been attracted to the celebrity status of Tim Horton, Joyce perceived the donut side of the business to be a sound retail concept where celebrity became secondary.[25] The hockey-star persona of the chain was downplayed, and Joyce's solid business management led to more franchises in the Hamilton area and ventures into real estate. There were 22 Tim Horton Donut shops in Ontario by late 1969, and Joyce was considering a move into the Toronto market. Confident that his partner had business matters under control, Horton turned his attention back to hockey.

CHANGE OF SEASONS

With a year left on his $42,000 a year contract, Tim informed the new Leafs General Manager, Jim Gregory, he would return for 1969-70 if his salary doubled. Although some contend he settled for $70,000, others claim that Ballard agreed to his terms.[26] Having spent the summer working on his business and then missing training camp, the 39-year-old defenseman was in poor shape and struggled early. "It takes considerable mental and physical preparation to get ready for a regular season. I didn't do either, of course," he told writer George Cross. "Now I'm taking a crash course in both, I'm finding out how out-of-shape I really am."[27]

Tim's struggles on the ice mirrored those of his team, a shadow of its former greatness. The last-place Maple Leafs traded their veteran to the New York Rangers on March 5, 1970, the first time he had ever been traded. Gregory knew that the deal would have a large impact on the team. "It had an emotional effect on me, too. I couldn't eat before the game, and I wasn't very hungry when I tried eating afterward." he told writer Dan Proudfoot. "The decision had to be Horton's. When a man has spent 23 seasons with an organization and performed the way Horton has, you just don't trade him."[28] Overcome with emotion, the defenseman could barely say goodbye to his teammates.

The Rangers were happy to add the veteran defenseman to its talented team. "He's been the class act down through the years, probably one of the best defensive defensemen in the league," said New York coach Emile Francis. "Who wouldn't love to have him?"[29] Playing much more conservatively in the twilight of his career, Horton helped to steady the blue line but the Rangers struggled to a fourth place finish in the East, losing to the Bruins in the first playoff round. He also endured marital struggles at this time, his wife Lori bothered by his prolonged absences from the home, his heavy drinking, and his dark moods. The couple underwent marriage counseling, and afterwards Horton promised to control his drinking.

RETURN TO PITTSBURGH

Tim did not receive a lot of ice time during the 1970-71 season, but he enjoyed his time in New York and often referred to it as the happiest season of his career. Having overcome depression, his wife Lori moved the rest of the family to the city, and daughter Jeri-Lynn started dating Ab DeMarco, one of her father's teammates. The Rangers posted 49 wins and finished second overall in the East, losing to Montreal in the semi-finals of the playoffs. Francis left Horton off the protected list after the veteran announced his retirement during the summer, but he was claimed in the intra-league draft by Pittsburgh General Manager Red Kelly, his former teammate "I'm a tired old man. I've had enough hockey," he claimed. "It would take a lot of inducing to make me play another year, but money is not the prime consideration."[30] With his wife's family still living in Pittsburgh area, however, Tim decided to join the Penguins, in part because he thought the city would provide Lori with a good support network.

The 1971-72 season was just a few weeks old when Horton broke his ankle in a game against Chicago. Hurting the same leg he had damaged in 1947 and again in 1955, the defenseman remained sidelined for a long time. Separating his shoulder soon after his return, Tim was finished for the season after only 44 games. The Penguins finished fourth in the West and lost their opening playoff round. After Kelly was fired over the summer, Horton found himself once again on the unprotected list and pondering retirement.

REUNION WITH PUNCH

Joining the NHL in 1970-71, the Buffalo Sabres almost immediately hired Punch Imlach as Coach and General Manager. The expansion team missed the playoffs its first two years, however, and wanted to acquire veteran talent at the 1972 intra-league draft. The league had just been raided by the rival World Hockey Association, so the choices were limited. Imlach decided to lure the 42-year-old Horton to Buffalo by offering him a $125,000 one-year contract. "I'm happy to have a guy of his stature on my team," the coach asserted. "I don't think he's a pound over his playing weight. Our rink is a little smaller than some and that will help, too."[31]

Tim was in good shape to start the season, and provided a steady influence for his much younger teammates. He helped the vastly improved Sabres record

88 points, up from 51 during the previous campaign, and the team made the playoffs for the first time in franchise history. Buffalo was defeated by eventual Cup-winner Montreal in the opening playoff round, but the season was considered an overall success. Horton was voted the club's most valuable player by his teammates.

Announcing his retirement again, Horton spent much of the summer of 1973 relaxing at his cottage near Huntsville. Joyce was running the Tim Donut business, leaving the veteran defenseman with some money and leisure time. Tim liked to spend money on fast cars and big boats, however, and cash was always needed for the donut business. Horton found it hard to resist Imlach's offer of a $150,000 one-year contract. Towards the end of training camp he decided to return for his 24th NHL season when Imlach gave him a $17,000 Italian-built Ford Pantera as a signing bonus. "It honestly wasn't the money," he asserted. "Maybe it's just a bad habit I've acquired. I like to play hockey. I have a long time ahead to sit behind the desk."[32]

THE LAST HURRAH

Lori Horton was not exactly thrilled with the European model sportscar given to her husband. She was well aware of his bad eyesight, his affinity for speeding cars, and his history of automobile accidents. "He drove like an idiot, and I was just as bad," she claimed. "He used to buy me a car, a Pontiac GTA (or) a Trans Am. He would have his, and I would have mine. We'd watch Laugh-in every Monday night with the kids, and then we'd race all the way back to Buffalo...And he'd be caught many times, and nobody would do anything about it. The police would let him go."[33] Both Jim Charade and Ron Joyce had refused to drive with him. Soon after Horton received the Pantera, he invited former teammate Eddie Shack over to his house for a show-and-tell. "He was so proud of that car... he came to me and said Shackie! Shackie! Look at my car," Shack remembered. "And it was just a little thing...and he goes, Look at the engine! Listen to the power!"[34]

Having worked hard at controlling his drinking, Horton played well in a limited role for the 1973-74 Sabres. Often excused from demanding workouts, his offensive contributions had dwindled but he provided tactical and emotional stability on the blue line. He celebrated his 44th birthday early in the season, but was shaken by his father's death days later. Tim then suffered a badly bruised and swollen jaw on February 20th, when struck by an errant slap shot at practice. Determined to play at Maple Leaf Gardens the next night, he convinced Imlach to let him drive the Pantera back to Toronto.

Many of Tim's family members attended the Gardens for what most believed would be his last game there. Horton was in severe pain during the warm-ups, and he feared a broken jaw. The late Bob Goldham, then working for Hockey Night in Canada, saw the veteran defenseman in the dressing room. "What's in your jaw? Doughnuts?" he joked. "Naw," Horton replied, "even my doughnuts aren't this hard!"[35]

The defenseman took several painkillers before the game, but they started to wear off late in the second period. He limped to the bench with a sore ankle, and asked team physician Dr. John L. Butsch to give him a painkiller shot. Butsch was concerned that Tim already had taken enough medicine, however, and refused. After just one shift, Horton sat the rest of the third period out. He was still chosen third star of the game, a Leafs victory, but was booed when he failed to appear for the obligatory skate around.

Exhausted and drowsy, he tried to convince rookie Paul Terbenche to join him on the team bus, for the ride back to Buffalo. Terbenche was spending the night with his parents, who were visiting out of town, so Horton decided to drive. "Normally Tim would have returned to Buffalo on the team bus, but after he hurt his jaw, we decided to let him drive to Toronto to get medication. Once he had the car in Toronto, naturally, he had to drive it back," Imlach recalled. "Tim had paid me enough dues that I could afford him a few favors, like letting him drive his own car if he didn't want to ride the bus. After the game, we also gave him permission to visit his family in Willowdale (in the suburbs, north of Toronto)."[36]

Driving his sports car to the Tim Donut office in Oakville, he was later found there by Joyce, his wife Teri and friend Layton Coulter. "Tim was sitting in our office, his coat on, an ice pack wrapped around his jaw, his driver's gloves on," Ron later recollected. "He was sitting in the dark with his feet up on the table, with a vodka and soda in his hand. And I laughed like hell. He said, *'Go ahead, laugh - I can't!'*"[37]

They talked to about 4 a.m., then Joyce tried to persuade his business partner to spend the night at his house in Burlington, before driving to a doctor's appointment in Buffalo the next day. Horton took more painkillers, and then announced that he would meet Joyce back at his house after locking up the office. Ron left in his Lincoln Town Car. "There was no traffic on the highway (the Queen Elizabeth Way)", he remembered. "I was going maybe 110. I saw him coming. I thought he'd be going pretty good. He went by me, and that's the last I saw of him."[38]

THE MYSTERY OF HORTON'S CAR CRASH

Joyce wondered why his friend had not stopped in Burlington, as planned. "He was seen leaving the road, heading into the (Plains Road) exit, and he touched the shoulder. There was a large cloud of dust - I've heard this report," he claimed. "My gut feeling is that he made the decision to go there (the house) but was going too fast to make the exit."[39] Horton then supposedly decided to continue driving on to St. Catherine's.

In the years following Tim's car crash, the Horton family collected circumstantial evidence of a considerable police presence near the crash site shortly before the incident. Lori noted that he was actually braking when his car left the road, perhaps to avoid a police roadblock set up to catch him speeding. She also claimed that a Regional Police Officer informed her about police cruisers near the Lake Street exit just before the accident. The owner of a Texaco gas station, located next to the accident site, allegedly recalled several police cruisers driving onto the highway just prior to the crash.[40]

The accident was witnessed by St. Catherine's OPP Constable Mike Gula, according to a news report at the time. Gula supposedly radioed that he was chasing a speeding "German sports car or Porsche" after being passed by it near the Lake Street exit. Horton was thrown from the car when it somersaulted, the report said, and landed over 100 feet away. He was found with a faint pulse, but died in the ambulance on the way to the hospital. The report also noted that the Burlington OPP had broadcast a special speeding car advisory over the police radio. In his book Open Ice: The Tim Horton Story, Douglas Hunter discussed the report's inconsistencies:

The accident had taken place at the Lake Street exit. If Tim had passed Gula's cruiser near the exit, he would have been past him in a blur. There would have been no time to Gula to give chase. The time between his first encounter with Tim and the accident would have been a matter of seconds. It sounded very much like Tim had been intercepted by police receiving advance warning from Burlington, and that the accident immediately followed.[41]

Joyce has remained confused as to how the speeding Pantera was fine on the highway, only for Tim to lose control on a straight stretch of road. While the police denied that a roadblock had been set up, Joyce believed there might have been flashing lights by the roadside. "He came around the corner at Ontario Street and he's on a straightaway. It makes sense that there were (police) cars there," he reasoned. "Probably the police were trying to slow him down. There's some thought he tried to run off and the front left end hit the storm sewer."[42]

Joyce has also asserted that Horton was not drunk that fatal night, contrary to popular belief. In great discomfort because of his fractured jaw, he was certainly not in a good mood. An autopsy report allegedly found little or no alcohol in his blood, just codeine from the painkillers. Douglas Hunter distilled the essentials of the tragedy:

> He was 44 years old and he had played two debilitating hours of professional hockey; he had been up all night; he had been drinking, probably not enough to impair someone like Tim, but enough to make him less than fully alert; and perhaps most important, he was in tremendous pain and indiscriminately taking painkillers to find some relief. The critical event of the night might well have been when he tossed back a couple of painkillers as he left for Tim Donut.[43]

It has been suggested that Horton's serious jaw ailment could have caused a blood clot moving to his brain, thus resulting in an embolism and unconsciousness. This scenario seems less likely, but what is more certain is that he probably would have survived the crash had he been wearing his seatbelt. The driver's side of the smashed Pantera was hardly crushed, the late Allan Stanley later noted, but the passenger side was quite damaged. This was probably caused when Tim's body struck the passenger door as he was being thrown from the car. Stanley speculated that his late friend's sports car hit a drainage culvert, causing it to flip. "The time of the morning he was driving, no traffic, he's got a fast car and no place to give it a blowout except in that stretch," Stanley surmised. "An accident is hardly an inch away."[44]

Shaken and guilt-ridden after having viewed the smashed Pantera, Punch Imlach pretty much saw it like Stanley did. "Right where the accident happened there is the slightest bend in the road. Tim must have driven by it a thousand times," Imlach figured. "The way the police saw it, one wheel just got off the road a few inches. He tried to get it back, with all that power and the car's quick response, but it rolled out of control through the median and into the lanes on the other side."[45] In retrospect, Imlach came to regret giving his defenseman the car. "I always wondered if I had given Tim something a little less exotic," he said, "if he might still be alive."[46] Lori Horton also felt guilty about the tragedy. "I always felt bad about that," she later admitted, "because I knew he was in pain, and I know he wouldn't let me drive the car in that much pain."[47]

THE SAD GOOD-BYE

Early the next morning Maple Leafs President Harold Ballard was informed of Horton's death during the annual shareholders meeting at Maple Leaf Gardens. "I remember him as a kid from St. Catherine's who came to the Maple Leafs organization in running shoes and a leather jacket. He was one of the few Protestants who played hockey at St. Michael's College," Ballard said, as he addressed the shareholders. "I've lost a great friend and hockey has lost a great player. Nothing anybody can say is too good for Tim. He died as an all-star - the same way he lived and played."[48] King Clancy, the Maple Leafs executive, remembered him as a dedicated athlete. "Nothing was too much for Tim. No task too great," Clancy declared. "There were no ifs, ands or buts. He did the job, injured or not."[49]

Shaken by the tragedy, several of Horton's former Leafs teammates recalled his dedication. "I never knew a player so steady. You always knew what Tim Horton was going to do. No flash, no polish, all hard work," Frank Mahovlich said. "You have no idea how hard he worked to get that doughnut business thriving. He had a lot of tough years in the beginning. Now, all that hard work was for what?"[50] George Armstrong also reminisced. "To me, no finer person or teammate ever lived," he said. "He was a quiet inspiration. He didn't talk much but made sense when he did."[51]

On the night after Tim's death, the Sabres reluctantly decided to proceed with a scheduled game at home against the Atlanta Flames. Black armbands were issued to players, and a minute of silence was observed after the national anthem. Goalie Dave Dryden was so shaken up that he did not dress, and Horton's defensive partner, young Jim Schoenfeld, sobbed uncomfortably. The game ended in a 4-4 tie. Although Buffalo would finish fifth in the Eastern Division that season, out of the playoffs, the young team bonded as a result of the tragedy. A year later the talented Sabres found themselves playing in the Stanley Cup finals, where they eventually lost to Montreal.

Memorial services for Horton were held at Jerret Funeral Home in Willowdale, but the funeral was postponed for a week so that players and employees from the Sabres could attend. Over 1,200 people were at the service, held at Oriole-York Mills United Church. They included NHL President Clarence Campbell, Harold Ballard, several former players from the Leafs, and representatives from every NHL club. The players and their wives wore black armbands, and the honor guard was comprised of eight uniformed Buffalo policemen and traffic duty officers. At the Buffalo Auditorium, Gordon Griggs delivered the moving eulogy:

> To Tim life was a gift from God. He gave of himself in the game of hockey more than was required of any athlete. He accepted the glory of a Stanley Cup with his family and friends. He accepted his gift of life, this brimming love that he possessed and shared with all those who could celebrate with him.[52]

The service was solemn and subdued, with many players visibly shaken. "When I saw him in the casket, it seemed like such a wrong place for him," said an emotional Schoenfeld. "There was no way that man should ever be confined to a box."[53] Pallbearers for the funeral were several of Tim's teammates from the glory days: Armstrong, Baun, Keon, Stanley, Dick Duck, and Bill Harris. Honorary pallbearers included Imlach, Kelly, Schoenfeld, Shack and Terbenche, among others. After all final respects were paid, Horton's body was then buried at York Cemetery, and just before departing the grounds Lori Horton gently placed a bouquet of yellow and white daisies on top of his gravesite.

LEGACY: AN ICONIC PLAYER AND NAME

Tim Horton left an enduring legacy as one of the greatest, most endurable defenseman in NHL history. Very few players have matched the 1,446 regular season games or 24 seasons that he played. He still holds the record for consecutive games played as a Leaf, and his four Stanley Cups and six All-Star Team selections compensate somewhat for his never having captured the Norris Memorial Trophy as top defenseman.

He was posthumously inducted into the Hockey Hall of Fame in 1977, one of the few graduates of St. Mike's College to ever achieve that exalted status. In 1978 the American Hockey League formally established The Tim Horton Memorial Trophy, awarded each year to the top two players on the league's Canadian teams. Horton's jersey number, 7, was never assigned again, and remains unofficially retired by the club. In 1995 it was finally retired by the Toronto Maple Leafs in a formal pre-game ceremony at Maple Leafs Gardens.

Horton's name continues on, as both his brother Gerry and youngest daughter Traci have sons named after him. The local arena in his hometown of Cochrane also bears his famous name. Several Tim Horton Camps for underprivileged children have been set up across Canada, and operated by the Tim Horton Children's Foundation, a non-profit group. The original camp near Parry Sound was not funded well, but subsequent camps have featured modern, first-class facilities. In 1994 Tim Donut Ltd. also established a fundraising day. Called Camp Day Canada, proceeds from the happening benefit needy children.

The Tim Horton Donut business has developed into one of the greatest success stories in Canadian franchising history. In 1973 there were 33 locations across Canada.[54] By the year 2003, there were over 2,000 stores established across the country, and the franchise had also set up numerous operations in the U.S. Over three million doughnuts were sold every day in North America, making co-founder Ron Joyce a very wealthy man.

By 2014 Tim Horton's was one of Canada's premier companies, with a significant international presence. Tim Horton never lived to see the success that the business became, of course, and a sad part of his legacy is that the Horton family never really benefited from the success of Tim Horton Donuts.

When Horton died his widow Lori inherited his ownership shares in the Tim Horton franchise business, but by the mid 1970s the widow was experiencing many personal problems. Emotionally distraught over the loss of her husband, Lori Horton became addicted to painkillers, and her growing financial problems led to an urgent need for cash. Eventually Lori sold her interests in the growing enterprise to Joyce for one million dollars.

Having beaten her demons, by 1990 Lori launched a lawsuit against Joyce, in an attempt to secure more money out of her previous deal to sell to him her franchise interests. In court she claimed that she was not of sound mind at the time the agreement was made. The lawsuit also focused on a share trust agreement that Joyce had made with Tim before his death, which gave either partner control of the business in the event the other died.

The lawsuit was prolonged and emotional for both sides, particularly with proceeds from a $10,000,000 business at stake. The lives of Lori and her four daughters were scrutinized during the trial proceedings, and Lori was often deeply hurt by the unnecessary accusations. Matters were further complicated by the marriage between Ron Joyce Jr. and Jeri-Lynn Horton, offspring of the former business partners. Ron Jr. and Jeri-Lynn met each other while both were working in the business, when Jeri-Lynn actually operated her own Tim Horton outlet.

During the lawsuit, family and friends of Tim Horton, as well as former teammates, became emotionally divided. Some of them supported Lori, while others did not. In 1993 the courts finally ruled on the course, siding with Joyce's position. Lori Horton lost most of her remaining life savings during that long trial, mostly on legal costs and lawyers fees. A few years later she died of heart failure.

Aside from his achievements as a businessman, Tim Horton is arguably best remembered as a one of pro hockey's most explosive yet durable defenseman, an ironman in the great tradition of the legendary Gordie Howe. "When you look at Tim, doing everything to the max, you wonder how a guy like him would have coped with growing old...it does seem fitting that he go out doing something all out. It really does," former defensive mate Jim Schoenfeld later added. "Whether it was playing in an old-timers' hockey game or whatever it might have been, I don't think I could see Tim as someone who was going to sit on a porch and rock away his golden years. He was going to be a doer until he was unable to do. Unfortunately, it came too soon for all of us."[55]

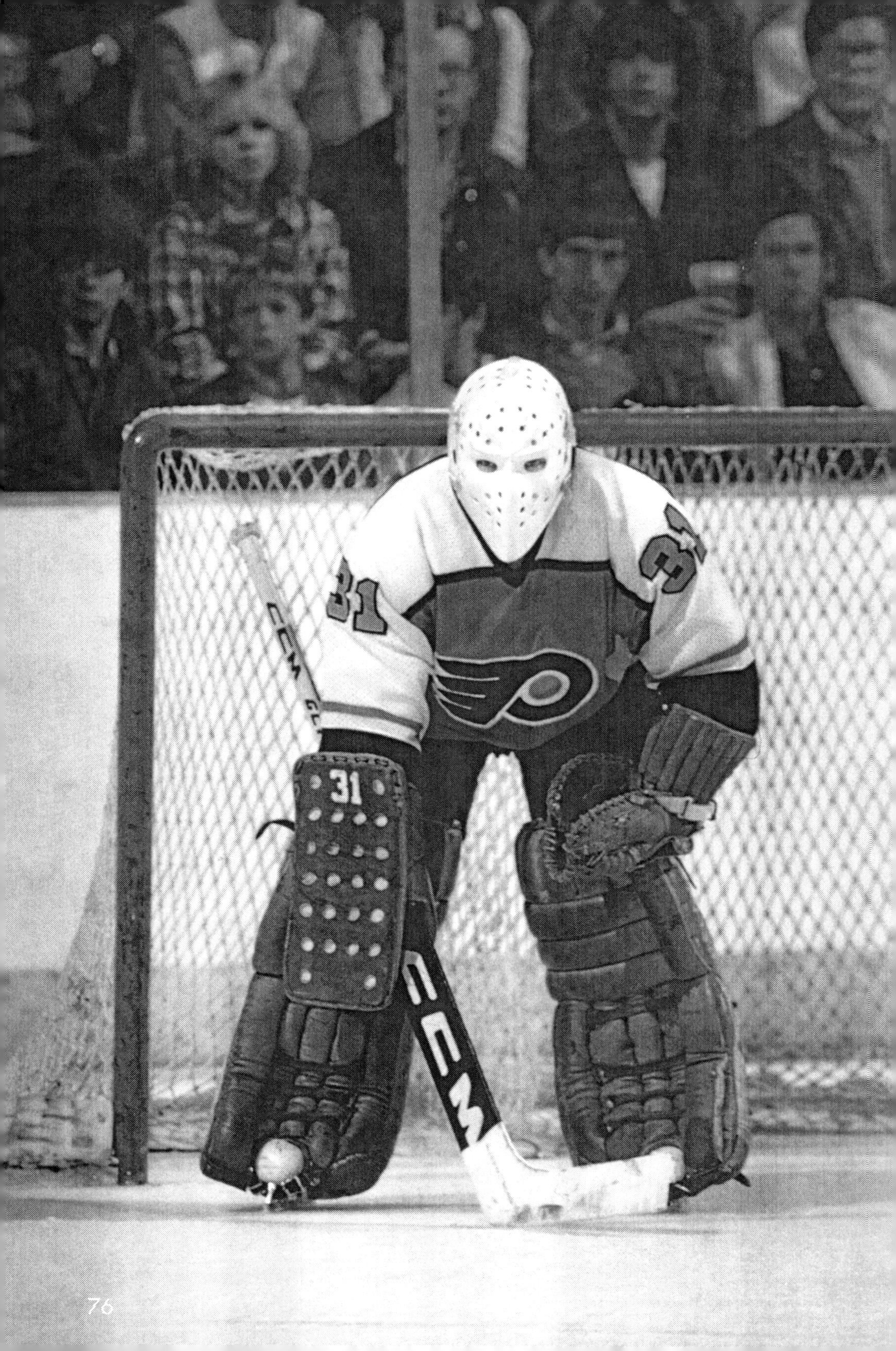
31
CCM

CHAPTER 4

1959 - 1985

PELLE LINDBERGH

Perhaps the most tragic hockey story of the 1980s concerned the high-speed car crash which claimed the talented young life of Pelle Lindbergh, the star Swedish goaltender of the Philadelphia Flyers. Having captured the Vezina Trophy as the National Hockey League's top goalie in 1985, Lindbergh seemed destined to become the first European goalie to not only star in, but to dominate the league. That enticing promise was abruptly cut short in the early morning hours of November 10, 1985, when he slammed his Porsche 930 sports car into the retaining wall of a New Jersey grade school. Declared brain dead at the hospital, Pelle was taken off life support just three days later. His death was mourned by the pro hockey world, especially those in the city of Philadelphia and the nation of Sweden, a stark reminder of the dangers of drinking and driving.

DREAMING OF THE NHL

Born May 24, 1959, in Stockholm, Sweden, Per-Erik Lindbergh was the third child and first son of Sigge and Anne-Lise Lindbergh. Determined that Per-Erik would enjoy ice hockey later on in life, Sigge signed his infant son up as a member of the local Hammarby IF athletic association. Growing up in a working class south Stockholm neighborhood, Pelle was surrounded by reminders of ice hockey's popularity in Sweden. By the age of four he was already skating and playing shinny, and the next Christmas Sigge presented his son with his first set of goalie pads and gloves.

Young Lindbergh was captivated with the World Hockey Championships, which he watched on television. "I remember a Canadian goalie named Seth

Martin, and I especially liked his mask," he later recalled. "After watching him play, I said to myself: 'that's what I want to do'. From the age of ten, it was my goal to become a professional goaltender."[1] He joined the boy's team at Hammarby later that year, and met his mentor, Carl Lindstrom, the future coach of the Swedish and Finnish national teams.

A very quick study at Hammarby, soon Pelle was the team's number one goalie. The league's top stopper by the age of 12, his strong positional play prompted coach Lindstrom to tell the netminder that he was destined for greatness. A few years later, in 1975, the coach arranged for Lindbergh to play with Team Stockholm-TV Pucken, a well kown boys' hockey club. The coach showed him Stanley Cup game films of Philadelphia Flyers goalie Bernie Parent, a future Hall of Fame goalie.

Instantly smitten by Parent's style, Lindbergh idolized the Flyers' great from then on, adopting the Flyers as his favorite NHL team. He copied Parent's stand-up positioning, his after-the-whistle mannerisms, and also had a goalie mask designed in the style of Parent's unique one, white with small eyeholes. Whereas Pelle's friends dreamed of suiting up for Landslaget, the famed Swedish National Team, Lindbergh was determined to some day star in the NHL.

Tending goal for the Swedish Junior National Team by age 17, he was voted top netminder at the European Junior Championships. Pelle played Division One hockey for Hammarby in 1978-79, but decided to further his hockey career the following season with Alk Elitserien of the Swedish Elite League.

A traditional powerhouse, the club had fallen on hard times by the late 1970s, having lost young stars like Thomas Gradin and Kent Nilsson to the NHL. In Pelle's first year, the team finished ninth, but the following season Lindbergh's steady, often spectacular netminding propelled the squad to a more respectable fifth place. In thirty-one games, he posted a 14-13-4 record and notched two shutouts. Then the netminder joined Sweden at the World Junior Championships, where he was selected the most outstanding goalkeeper.

Scouts from the Flyers were closely watching Pelle's success in Europe; having never replaced the retired Bernie Parent, the club was searching for a young talented goalie who could blossom into the star that would help Philadelphia recapture its glory days. Lindbergh was chosen in the second round of the 1979 entry draft by the Flyers, after their top first-round pick, Canadian junior star Brian Propp. He was absolutely surprised and elated to be selected by his favorite team, having been unaware of the interest in him. Confident and enthusiastic, he led Sweden to a Bronze Medal at the 1980 Olympics in Lake Placid, New York; Sweden was the only team not to have been defeated by the Gold Medalist Americans. During the high-scoring tournament, he compiled a 3.66 goals-against-average in five games. In February, Sports Radio Sweden voted him the country's athlete of the month.

FROM SWEDEN TO PHILADELPHIA

When Pelle joined the Philadelphia Flyers organization just prior to 1980-81, he soon realized the obstacles and stereotypes he needed to overcome in the NHL. Several foreign-born players had come into the league, but no European goalkeeper had ever won a regular job, let alone a starting position. In the 1970s Swedish netminders such as Christian Abrahamsson and Leif Honken Holmqvist were never seriously considered for regular spots on NHL squads, and ultimately ended up toiling in the renegade World Hockey Association.

Hardy Astrom was the Swede with the most NHL experience, but he compiled a rather poor record of 15-42-12 over parts of three forgettable seasons with the New York Rangers and the Colorado Rockies. He shared starting goalie duties in his last year in Colorado, advancing no further. Lindbergh would have to be an historic trend-setter if he entertained notions of becoming the Flyers' goalie of the future.

Pelle's tour in Philadelphia's system began in the minor leagues, and it was a very successful stint. In 1980-81, with the Flyers' top farm club, the Maine Mariners of the American Hockey League, he played fifty-one games, posting a solid 31-14-5 record with the powerful team. He was voted rookie-of-the-year, selected to the First All-Star Team, and shared the Hap Holmes Trophy for top netminding honors with back-up Robbie Moore. Lindbergh was also voted as the AHL's Most Valuable Player, a rare feat for any netminder. He then had a stellar playoffs, compiling a 10-7 record to lead the Mariners to the Calder Cup title. Management was now convinced that they had found their star goalie.

Playing for Sweden at the 1981 Canada Cup championship in the autumn, he faced the top NHL and international snipers. Although he allowed eight goals in two games, both losses, he had fared decently against NHL shooters, and the learning experience made him more confident and certain that he belonged in the big league. He was already being recognized as undoubtedly the best goaltending talent to ever come out of Sweden, and the future looked very bright for the twenty-one-year-old.

Again apprenticing with Maine the following season, Lindbergh had a 17-7-2 record and a goals-against-average of 3.31, impressive for such a high-scoring league. His steady play had kept the Mariners among the elite of the AHL, and Philadelphia's management took even more notice of the star developing in their farm system. Pelle was called up to the parent club late in the regular campaign, but spent most of his time on the bench, backing up Pete Peeters, who had suddenly and rather surprisingly emerged as one of the NHL's best netminders. Playing in just eight games, Lindbergh was 2-4-2 with a 4.38 goals-against-average.

Pelle was twenty-three years old in 1982-83, and the Flyers' organization was convinced that he was ready to play regularly in the NHL. Philadelphia was suddenly quite strong between the pipes, with the capable Peters backed up by veteran Rick St. Croix, Lindbergh and Bob Froese, another hot young prospect. Deciding to go with their young netminders, the club traded Peeters to Boston for defenseman Bob McCrimmon early in the season.

Lindbergh badly outplayed St. Croix early on, quickly earning the starting position. He bore an uncanny resemblance to the great Parent, with his white mask and its small eyeholes, and this immediately endeared him to Flyers fans. During the regular schedule, Pelle notched three shutouts, and compiled a 23-13-3 record with an impressive 2.98 goals-against-average. Even more noticeable were the statistics of talented Bob Froese, who had been recalled from Maine and registered a 17-4-2 record with a sparkling 2.52 goals-against-average.

Together the two netminders led Philadelphia to a first-place finish in the highly competitive Patrick Division, but the Swede started in goal for the opening playoff round against the New York Rangers. Pelle was shaky from the onset, allowing eighteen goals in three games as the Rangers swept Philadelphia in the five-game series. He retreated to Sweden in the off-season, keeping himself in shape by playing local hockey, and looking forward to redeeming himself the following season.

The Swedish goalie returned to Philadelphia and the starting goalie job in 1983-84, but he struggled so much with his confidence and play that he lost the number one position to upstart Froese. In thirty-six games, Pelle had one shutout, with an unimpressive 16-13-3 record and 4.05 goals-against-average. Sent down to the Springfield Indians of the AHL late in the season, he promptly reeled off four straight wins, allowing only twelve goals, and regained some of his former cockiness.

Lindbergh was then called up just before the start of the NHL post-season, but the third-place Flyers decided to start Froese in the opening series. Once again, the Flyers exited early, in spite of employing both young goalies. Appearing in just two games, Pelle was 0-1 with an inflated 6.92 goals-against-average. Doubts were starting to surface, both within the Flyers' organization and around the NHL, as to whether the young Swedish talent had the mental toughness to defy the stereotypes about European goalies, and become an NHL star.

A STAR IS BORN

Lingering questions about Pelle Lindbergh's abilities were promptly cast aside during the Flyers' training camp in the fall of 1984. Badly outperforming Froese in the pre-season, the Swede effectively stole the number one job back before the regular campaign began. The opportunity provided to Lindbergh to prove himself all over again was engineered by a changing of the guard within the organization.

Having decided to phase himself out of the club's daily operations, long-time owner Ed Snider installed his capable son Jay as the President. Keith Allen, the General Manager, was kicked upstairs, replaced by the team's recently retired star captain, Bobby Clarke. Clarke gave Pelle the chance to show his stuff, and also hired fiery young Mike Keenan as coach, to motivate the league's youngest squad.

These sweeping management changes lit a fire under the players, and produced immediate results on the ice. The Keenan-coached Flyers were the hottest NHL team out of the gate, the players driven as much by the fear of Iron Mike as anything. For most of 1984-85 Philadelphia led the league standings, eventually finishing first in the Patrick Division. It was Lindbergh's best, and last full, NHL season. He led all goalies in games played, 65, and in wins. He posted a sizzling 40-17-7 record, and recorded two shutouts and a 3.05 goals-against-average. Pelle was also selected to the First All-Star Team, the first Swede so honored since former Maple Leaf Borje Salming. He capped off an incredible year by capturing the Vezina Trophy as best goalie, the first European netminder to ever win the Vezina or any NHL award.

His selection to play in the 1985 all-star game at mid-season marked the first time a European goalie had participated in the classic contest. He allowed eight goals during the high-scoring contest, four of them to game MVP Wayne Gretzky, and later joked that he could not have stopped a beach ball that night. That year he was also the first goalkeeper to regularly place a water bottle on top of his net, a regular practice in today's pro hockey. Back in 1984-85, opponents were often amused by this.

Pelle's impressive statistics did not tell the whole story. Philadelphia was an exciting, young hockey team, which played with a lot of emotion, but the squad was often undisciplined and prone to losing its composure. Lindbergh's solid, often superlative goaltending was invariably the glue that held the temperamental club together. He was repeatedly called upon to stop numerous two-on-one and three-on-two rushes, caused largely by inopportune offensive risks by unseasoned defensemen. His young teammates often took needless penalties, requiring Pelle to bail them out of countless five-on-three shorthanded situations.

Pelle's 3.05 goals-against-average might seem a bit high by today's standards, particularly for a Vezina Trophy winner, but it must be placed within the context of the offensive, high-scoring contests which defined NHL hockey in the mid-1980s. The league featured explosive, talented teams like the Edmonton Oilers, led by Gretzky, Jari Kurri and Paul Coffey, and the rules clearly favored offense over defense. By the early 1990s, the NHL had adopted a more defensive style of play, and has not since recaptured the excitement and electricity of that goal-hungry era.

Lindbergh's confident, steady play backstopped the inexperienced but motivated squad all the way to the 1985 Stanley Cup finals, where they faced off against the Edmonton Oilers, defending champions and already well on their way to becoming a full-fledged hockey dynasty. Most hockey observers expected the young Flyers squad to be easy fodder for the Oilers, an offensive machine finishing first in the offensive-minded Smythe Division. Pelle stole the first game almost all by himself. He repeatedly turned back the likes of Gretzky and Kurri, and allowed his teammates to counter-punch effectively. Philadelphia managed a 4-1 win. Edmonton coach Glen Sather was visibly angry after the upset, and lashed out at the Swedish goalie's habit of placing his water bottle on the back of his cage. "The next thing they'll be doing," Sather sarcastically quipped, "is getting room service for a chicken dinner out there."[2]

The Oilers eventually proved too powerful for the overmatched Flyers, winning the next four games to capture its second straight Stanley Cup. With his strong post-season performance, however, Lindbergh had broken the playoff jinx. His 12-6 record and superb 2.50 goals-against-average earned him serious consideration for the Conn Smythe Trophy as Most Valuable Player in the playoffs, but the award was captured by hockey's premier superstar, Wayne Gretzky.[3]

Pelle experienced one of his finest moments when he was presented the Vezina Trophy at the NHL Awards Ceremony in Toronto on June 13, 1985. The Swedish netminder was presented the award by his boyhood idol, Bernie Parent. As the team's goaltending coach, Parent had not only become a mentor but also a close friend of the young European prodigy who grew up in awe of him. In a moving acceptance speech before pro hockey's elite, Lindbergh dedicated the Vezina to his childhood hero.

PARTY IN NEW JERSEY

Having spent the off-season resting and visiting family and friends in Sweden, Pelle returned to Philadelphia rejuvenated and eager to continue his winning ways in 1985-86. He won six of his first eight games, recording a solid 2.88

goals-against-average. The Flyers were off to a great start, led by the solid play of both Froese and Lindbergh. On November 6th in Chicago, Pelle led Philadelphia to their ninth straight win, 6-2 over the Black Hawks. In their next game, at home on November 9th against the Bruins, coach Keenan rested his star Swedish goalie and started Froese. Philadelphia posted a 5-3 victory, their tenth straight, and afterwards most of the players, in a celebratory mood, gathered at an after-hours club adjacent to the Flyers' practice facility, the Coliseum, in nearby Vorhees, New Jersey.

Pelle did not immediately attend the party at the club, deciding instead to drive his sedan back home, to King's Grant in Morton, New Jersey, where he resided with Kerstin Pietzsch, his Swedish fiancee. His good friend Ed Parvin and some of his friends from Sweden, visiting the United States, were already at the club. Parvin knew many players well, since his father was the real estate agent who sold many of them their homes. Ed telephoned the goalie at home, inviting him down to the bar. Lindbergh told him he would be down shortly, kissed Kerstin good-bye, and then left in his custom-made, red Porsche turbo, leaving the dependable Sedan at home.

The Swedish netminder's red Porsche turbo was his pride and joy; having cost over one million SEK ($125,000 in U.S.) and boasting a 565-horsepower engine, the sleek sports car was built for speed. Lindbergh loved to drive fast; back in Sweden, he was known for racing his speed boat around the coast of Stockholm each summer. Both Kerstin and his mother disdained his often insatiable appetite for fast, reckless driving. "He loved cars," former teammate and close friend Rick Tocchet recalled. "He had the fastest Porsche in South Jersey."

When Pelle arrived at the after-hours club, the party was in full swing. The Flyers players were relaxed and in the mood to drink as they entered a five-day layoff on the heels of their winning streak. Lindbergh and several teammates hung around longer than they had originally planned to and consumed way too much alcohol. Pelle finally called Kerstin around 5 a.m., and told her he was on his way home. He offered a ride to Ed Parvin and his girlfriend, Kathy McNeal; the pair had received a ride to the Coliseum, but had not arranged a return trip home. Readily accepting the offer, the couple headed off with the goalie to the Porsche.

THE ACCIDENT

It was 5:20 a.m., and Pelle was behind the wheel of his beloved car. His passengers should have noticed that he was clearly drunk; blood-tests results would later show his blood-alcohol level to range from 0.17 to 0.24, well above the 0.10 reading which was New Jersey's legal limit. Parvin climbed into the passenger side of the two-seat Porsche, and McNeal squeezed into the middle, between the two men, around the console. While the sports car was a state-of-the-art machine, it was not known for having a lot of space inside, so the three did not have much room to maneuver.

About ten minutes into the drive home, the speeding Porsche hurtling down a residential road in Somerdale, New Jersey, Lindbergh lost control of the vehicle as he negotiated a steep curve. With his judgment severely impaired and his reflexes much too slow, the Flyers goalie was unable to stop the sliding sports car from crashing almost head-on into a retaining wall, in front of Somerdale Elementary School.[4]

Area residents rushed out to the accident scene upon hearing the thunderous crash, and tried their best to help the accident victims. A call to 911 was placed, and an ambulance arrived on the scene within 15 to 20 minutes. Betty-Ann Cowling was one of the first emergency medical technicians there, and later told the press that Pelle's car was southbound on Somerdale Road when it slammed into a cement wall, after crossing the northbound lane.

The accident occurred on a sharp curve that had been the site of several past accidents. Cowling recalled that the driver's side of the vehicle was crushed by the impact, the entire hood having peen pushed into the seat area, and that the "jaws-of-life" were used to open the passenger door.[5]

All three crash victims suffered extensive injuries, but Pelle's were by far the worst. Although he had a pulse, he had suffered a badly broken leg and was bleeding from the nose and mouth. Lindbergh also incurred massive brainstem trauma; the brain stem, which controls the oxygen flow to the brain, was injured so badly that he actually went into cardiac arrest while he being moved, but was resuscitated. Pelle had stopped breathing 15 minutes before the emergency crew arrived and again in the ambulance, as he was rushed to John F. Kennedy Hospital in nearby Stratford. He didn't resume breathing until placed on a respirator in the emergency room, 15 minutes later. The lack of oxygen "damaged the brain secondarily," noted Flyers team physician Dr. Edward Viner soon after, "so we have a very, very grave situation."[6] He was promptly placed on life support by doctors.

The other passengers in the car did not suffer nearly as extensive damage. Taken to the same hospital as the Flyers goalie, McNeal was in stable condition, with minor liver, pelvis and spleen problems. Parvin was transported to another infirmary, where he was treated for skull compression fracture and lay in a coma for ten days.

Many of Pelle's teammates were at the hospital shortly afterwards, joining those already there: the late Flyers sportscaster Gene Hart, coach Keenan, Kerstin and Anne-Lise Lindbergh, Pelle's mother, who was visiting her son from Sweden. Doctors soon delivered the bad news – the goalie was brain dead, breathing only with the help of a respirator.

After the hospital, most players went to the training rink, the Coliseum in nearby Voorhees, for a meeting. "It was felt they should all be together and told what has happened," said Flyers spokesman Rodger Gotlieb. "They're all very shaken. It's a tragedy of the most overwhelming proportions."[7] Within hours the local press had broadcast details of the crash, and several fans gathered outside the hospital to hold prayer vigils for the stricken netminder.

There was immediate speculation that Lindbergh was driving drunk. "It is conceivable that alcohol had something to do with this accident, and the hope for recovery is really nil," Dr. Viner conceded. "He had been drinking. I really feel very, very ambivalent about what to say about this. Obviously he had something to drink. This is not a young man that was out drinking all the time. For Pelle to have a beer or two was the most we ever saw."[8]

For a few days the Lindbergh family grappled with the emotional issue of eventually having to agree to disconnect Pelle's life support. "We can't do anything about making that kind of decision," Gotlieb noted, "until they come to grips with this."[9] After Sigge Lindbergh arrived from Sweden, the family bid a tearful farewell before the respirator was turned off. His essential organs – cornea, heart, liver, kidneys – were donated, and ended up saving the lives of seriously-ill people. "It was," Keenan later claimed, "Pelle's finest – and greatest – save."[10]

MOURNING LINDBERGH

Lindbergh's unexpected and sudden death stunned the hockey world, particularly in Philadelphia and his native Sweden. "Just the shock of losing Pelle the way we did is going to hit this club very, very hard," admitted one Flyer, who requested anonymity. "It's going to be bloody difficult to concentrate on hockey for a long time."[11]

Flyers General Manager Bobby Clarke noted that Pelle was personable as well as a great goalie, and an inspiration to his teammates. "He liked to drive fast and we had told him repeatedly to slow down. But I suppose when you're young, strong and full of life you think you're invulnerable to everything. I guess it's natural to feel that nothing can ever happen to you," Clarke admitted. "It's going to take a couple of days for this to sink in. We do know that it's an enormous loss for his family and our hockey club. We haven't made any decisions on our goaltending or any other part of it."[12]

For the first two days after the accident, most Flyers players went to coach Keenan's house, trying to make sense of the tragedy. Many also often gathered at the home of team captain Dave Poulin, mostly to share their common grief and to gather strength. There the team developed a special bond. "When we got together... nowadays you might get four guys. We had eighteen guys there," Rick Tocchet later recalled. "That's the type of team we had. We were very close. That's the closest I've ever been on a team. We won a lot of games because of the chemistry, not the talent."[13] The meetings at Poulin's house were therapeutic for several young players. "They were essentially group therapy sessions," said Poulin. "Talking things out that usually go unexpressed and would have remained unexpressed had we been alone. We knew the character of this team. We knew how we all felt about one another. But a lot of those feelings had never been expressed, not just because we're athletes, but because we're males. As much as Pelle's death pulled us together, I think it showed how close we already were."[14]

News of Lindbergh's death also shocked the Swedish hockey world, where the goalie was considered a pioneer in the sport. "This is very, very bad news. I'm very sorry to hear of this and I know most of the Swedish people will be very sorry. He played for our national team and he was certainly an attraction, the way he played," said Bjorn Wagnnson, the agent who signed Pelle to his first Flyers contact. "When the players leave here to play in the NHL, they're already big stars and they're well known. Pelle was quite a star because of the season he had in the NHL last year."[15]

Curt Lindstrom, then coach of the Swedish national hockey team, told the press he had talked to the goalie just weeks earlier. "I first met Pelle when he was only eight and I coached him in on one of Hammarsby's cub teams," he remembered. "He was a fantastic guy in all respects. He was something of a child prodigy. We soon discovered his phenomenal talent as a goaltender even at that tender age. He also remained the same nice kid throughout despite his success, always smiling, friendly, open and positive."[16]

TRIBUTES TO A SWEDISH STAR

There were two funeral services honoring Pelle Lindbergh, one held in North America, the other in Sweden. Held on November 14th, the day after Pelle was taken off life support, the first mass was at Gloria Die Church (Old Swede's Church) in Philadelphia. In attendance were the Flyers players and management, as well as representatives from the NHL and all the league's teams.

The congregation was addressed with an emotional, heartfelt eulogy from the team captain. "Pelle was a terrific competitor with an unmatched will to win," Poulin declared. "Anything he did he had to be the best at, and through his exuberance and personality, he transmitted that to us. He wasn't happy unless there was something on the line."[17]

Philadelphia was scheduled to play the Edmonton Oilers at the Spectrum later that night. Printed well before Lindbergh's death, tickets for the game eerily displayed a game action photo of the recently deceased goalie. Out of respect for Lindbergh, the Flyers organization instructed ticket handlers at the gates not to tear the stubs in half, as was the normal procedure, but to simply mark the back with black marker. Memorial cards bearing Pelle's image were also printed for the game, and handed out to fans entering the arena. A special pre-game tribute had both the players from both teams line up on their respective bluelines, as Gene Hart delivered a moving, yet emotionally calming speech in Lindbergh's memory. Sigge Lindbergh visited the Flyers dressing room after the game; unable to speak much English, the elder Swede simply offered a firm handshake to each of his late son's teammates.

Special tributes were also held around the Swedish Elite League that night, and before its next home game the Hammarsby hockey club announced the establishment of The Pelle Lindbergh Memorial Fund. The late goalie's remains were flown to Sweden right after memorial services in Philadelphia, and another memorial mass was held at Sofia Church, south of Stockholm, where Pelle and his bride-to-be had planned to marry the following summer. Subdued ceremonies were attended by Kerstin, the Lindberghs, other family members and various representatives from the Flyers, the NHL and the Swedish Elite League.

The church was filled to capacity, with another 200 to 300 hundred people gathered outside to follow the funeral proceedings. Towards the end of the service a friend of the Lindbergh family, Viki Benkert, sang Your Song, an Elton John melody which Pelle really liked.[18]

Philadelphia continued to play well in the aftermath of their goaltender's death. "The way they've faced the tragic loss of someone they loved and respected has been an inspiration to everyone in the community," coach Keenan asserted soon after. "The tragedy didn't really add to this team's character. The character was already there. The only difference is that now it is public."[19] Poulin noted that the players were trying to stay positive. "Despite the tragedy, this team is happy. Mike is a player's coach," he noted, "Everything Keenan does is designed to make it easier for us to keep our minds on hockey."[20]

Defenseman Brad Marsh was particularly confident of Philadelphia's abilities on the ice. "The saddest part is we're going to go on and win a couple of Cups," he reckoned, "and Pelle's going to miss that."[21] The Flyers finished first in the Patrick Division but lost in the division semi-finals; they made it to the Stanley Cup Finals the following season, 1986-87, yet never managed to re-capture that elusive Cup.

A SURVIVOR'S STORY

More than 15 years after the tragic accident, it remained hard for Ed Parvin to remember much about that fateful night. Having spent ten days in a coma after the incident, he awoke in the hospital with no memory of how he got there, only to be informed by his father that he had been in a horrific crash. His dad did not tell him what happened to his friend, and Parvin did not find out until weeks later, when Kerstin visited. "I asked her where Pelle was," he recalled, "and that's when I found out."[22]

Parvin still feels the lingering effects of the accident. "Sometimes when I get excited, my speech becomes jumbled," he admitted. "The part of my brain that was damaged was the part that controls my speech. I had speech therapy for about one and a half years."[23] Parvin considered Lindbergh a good friend, having even visited him in Sweden the summer prior to the tragedy, and has never blamed him for his current physical problems. "Things happen. He was a great guy and a great goalie," he claimed. "That (accident) was before all the (emphasis on) drinking and driving. It's different now. I think I would feel a lot worse if I had been driving."[24]

He also recently admitted that he still enjoys watching the Flyers play, but also conceded that his first visit to the Spectrum after the mishap was somewhat unnerving. "I really didn't comprehend (the scope of the tragedy) until I went to a Flyers game a few months later," he said. "Suddenly, I thought 17,000 people were looking at me."[25] Gradually putting the tragedy into perspective over the years, he has recently talked of how much he now values life. "I went to an Elton John concert awhile back and when he played Your Song, I remembered how much Pelle liked that," he said. "(Kerstin) played it at the funeral. (Hearing it again) kind of brought it all back again."[26]

Kathy McNeal recovered fully from the accident, according to Parvin at the time, and was living in California when he had last heard from her, while Kerstin Pietzsch moved back to Sweden, where she is now said to be married with children.

TEAMMATES REMEMBER LINDBERGH – 15 YEARS LATER

"It was really devastating," former Flyer Brian Propp recently recalled. "Pelle was a such a likeable guy...I've been to the school and looked at that wall, the angle the car struck at (where the wall separates for steps), if it had hit five feet either way, it would caromed off, but it just stuck there."[27] Propp, who later found work as a sportscaster for the team, believed Pelle was destined for great things. "I remember the year before, he had 40 wins. He was playing great hockey," Propp said. "In a couple more years, he would have been one of the best goaltenders in the NHL."[28]

"He used to talk about a fast boat he had in Sweden," Propp continued, discussing Lindbergh's love of speed. "But usually he was very, very careful with drinking. He wasn't really a big drinker at all.[29] Brian keeps a wallet-sized photo of his late teammate tucked into a lower corner of his bedroom mirror. "It's just to remind me that I had a special thing with Pelle. We had a mutual respect for each other. In practice, I would try to score on him, and he would try to stone me," he recalled. "There would be a smile and a wink and an I got you this time. Everyone got along with him, but I had something special with him. I was very fortunate that I was able to carry on and have a great life. It (the photo) reminds me of how fortunate we really are."[30]

"I was only 19, 20 years old at the time, and it hit me real hard," recalled Rick Tocchet. "I remember thinking `what a waste'. Everyone remembers he was a great goalie but he was also a great guy. That's what sticks in my head."[31] Tocchet was traded away by Philadelphia in 1992, but the veteran found himself back with the club eight years later. At 36 he reflected on just how much time had passed since Lindbergh's death. "They have some new pictures up in the First Union Center now, and just the other day I noticed one of Pelle and Bernie together," he said. "I was really young then. What I remember most is that for two days, we just stayed at Mike Keenan's house, having what I guess you would call therapy sessions. Then on Thursday after it happened, we played Edmonton at the Spectrum. That was a pretty emotional game."[32]

By 2000 there were few remaining holdovers from that 1985 Flyers team – one was Jim "Turk" Evers, the equipment manager. Evers has never handed out Pelle's number 31 to any other player since the tragedy, although the team had not yet officially retired it. "One guy - Nick Little - asked for it when he first got here. He didn't know and he was okay with it when I explained it to him," Jim recalled. "Pelle was a team person, always in a good mood, always joyful… I live near that school now, and I drive past that wall every day on the way to work, and I still get goose bumps."[33]

LEGACY: THE SWEDISH PHENOM

After Lindbergh's death, the Philadelphia Flyers left his dressing room stall intact for the remainder of the season, a small Swedish flag placed on top of the empty locker. The club established a special team award in his name; each year The Pelle Lindbergh Memorial Trophy is still awarded to the most improved player.

Many current NHL players would have trouble recalling much about the late Flyers goalie, but former Philadelphia netminder Brian Boucher actually remembered watching Pelle play on television, in a game against the Bruins. "I know he wore a white mask with the eyeholes," said Boucher, who was only eight when the Swedish star died, "and he wore number 31."[34]

Perhaps Lindbergh may be more aptly thought of as a true pioneer of the game, the first star European netminder. "He was the first Swedish goaltender to go over to the NHL and be a big star," noted Wagnnson. "Everybody expected him to be one of the greatest goalies in NHL history."[35] Pelle compiled a dominant 87-49-15 record in his brief NHL tenure, earning a First All-Star Team nod and the Vezina Trophy as top goalie. His unprecedented success paved the way for other European cagers to star in the NHL, such as Dominik Hasek and Nikholai Khabibulin. It seems, however, that tragedy truly diminished Lindbergh's potential legacy, as he was destined to be more than simply a European pioneer. Instead of being one of the greatest goalies in NHL history, Pelle Lindbergh will probably be remembered as the rising Swedish star whose unfulfilled promise was tragically cut short by his love of speed.

In the wake of Pelle Lindbergh's tragic death the Philadelphia Flyers have never been able to ride a goaltender all the way to Stanley Cup victory. They managed to solve their problems between the pipes with Ron Hextall, who as a rookie in 1986 back stopped the team all the way to the Stanley Cup finals, where he won the Conn Smythe Trophy as playoff MVP even as the

Flyers lost to Wayne Gretzky's Oilers. Hextall helped return the Flyers to the finals eleven years later, but the team was swept by the Red Wings. In 2010 it was Brian Boucher's turn, but Philadelphia dropped that finals series in a hard fought battle with the Black Hawks.

Much has changed in the city of brotherly love since the autumn of 1985, when tragedy struck Pelle Lindbergh and the Philadelphia Flyers. Some two decades later the Flyers are still searching for the star goaltender who will help them deliver that third Stanley Cup. It is little wonder, then, that Flyers fans past and present look back with nostalgia to the early 1980s, when their beloved Pelle looked poised on making good on the dream. It all ended with a fatal car accident, however, leaving many to only imagine what great hockey triumphs might have been on the horizon for their beloved star Swedish goalie and his orange-and-black clad teammates.

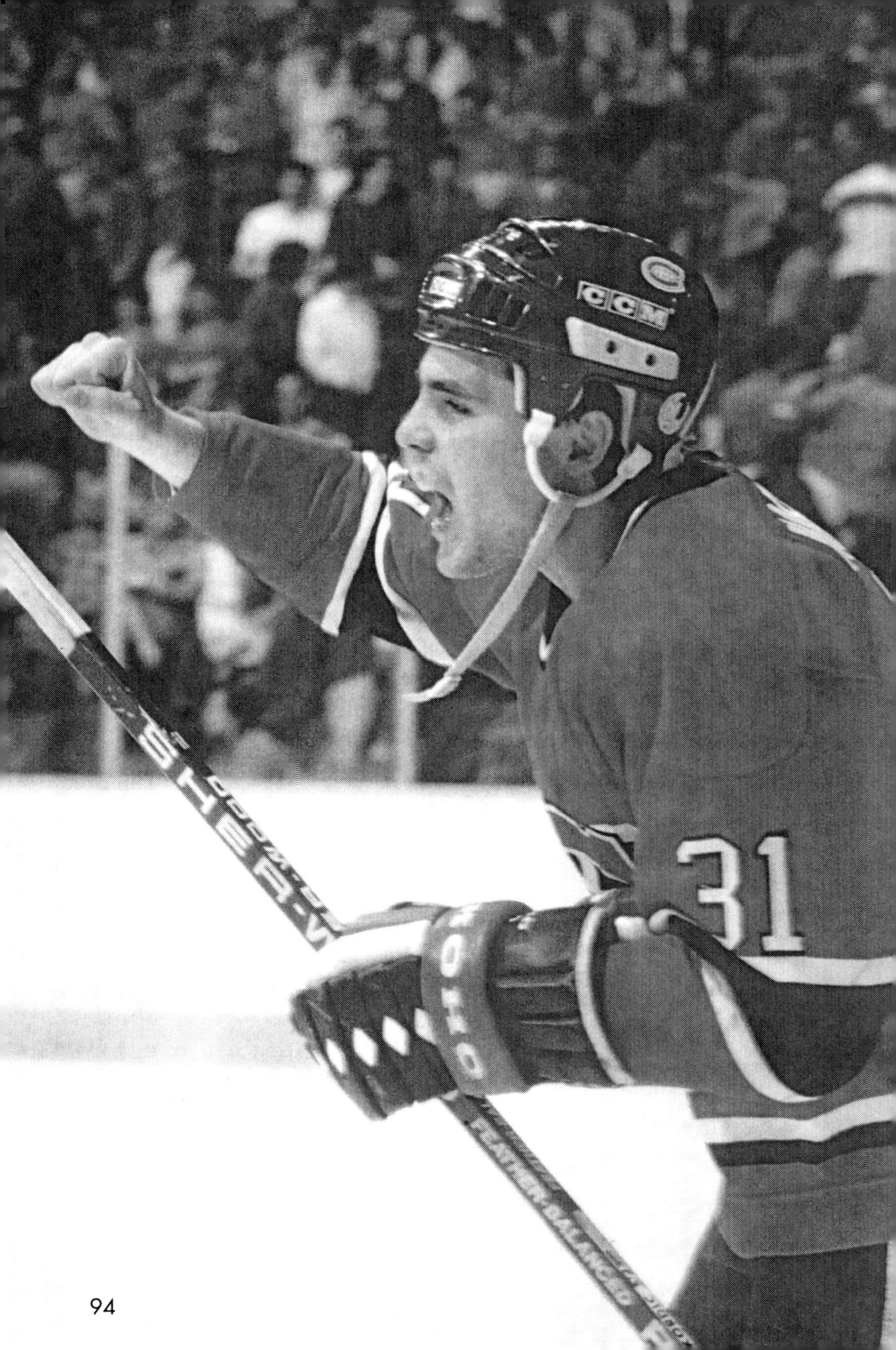
CCM
31

CHAPTER 5

1965 - 1992

JOHN KORDIC

On April 8, 1992, pro hockey's perennial bad boy and enforcer, 27-year-old John Kordic, died on the way to the hospital after a violent struggle with several Quebec City police officers. Police had tried to restrain the enraged hockey player in his Quebec City motel room. The coroner's office eventually concluded that Kordic's death resulted from an aggravated physical state brought on by ingestion of a large amount of cocaine, and somewhat promoted by strong-armed police intervention. The public inquiry, however, stopped short of accusing the police of criminal wrongdoing, and the Kordic family launched a $1.6 million lawsuit against the police, the ambulance service, and the city of Quebec. The suit was settled out of court, but questions remained regarding possible law enforcement negligence, and a subsequent cover-up.

The NHL developed a more comprehensive substance-abuse policy for its players in the aftermath of the Kordic tragedy, in recognition of the competitive pressures in pro sports which often compel some athletes to abuse alcohol and drugs. Kordic's own substance abuse has been largely linked to his feelings of low self-esteem, in light of his inability to please his father, angry that his son was known for fighting rather than playing hockey.

GROWING UP IN EDMONTON

In 1963, Ivan and Regina Kordic emigrated from Croatia to Western Canada, settling in Edmonton, Alberta, where Ivan plied his trade as a skilled cabinet maker. Two years later, on March 25, 1965, John was born, to be later followed by siblings Toni, Dan and Lillian. The Kordic household was steeped in traditional values, and Ivan Kordic installed a sense of respect for the teachings of the Bible in all four of his chidren.[1]

As a young boy Kordic loved to draw and paint with oils, and displayed impressive artistic talent. On Saturday evenings he watched Hockey Night in Canada on CBC-TV with his father, an avid hockey fan who better appreciated the sport's skill rather than the violence. In the winter John played shinny hockey on frozen ponds near his house, wearing number 4 in tribute to his idol, Boston's great Bobby On. His favorite team was still the Maple Leafs, however, and he particularly liked Darryl Sittler and Dave "Tiger" Williams, the latter a rugged enforcer.

Kordic graduated from the outside rinks to organized minor-league hockey, and by the age of 16 he was a strapping 5 foot 11, 180-pound defenseman with The Knights of Columbus, a bantam A-level entry. The mobile defender also played local soccer as a goalkeeper, and was good enough to be actively recruited by the Edmonton Drillers of the Canadian Soccer League.[2]

The coach of his bantam A team, Percy Kozak, liked the skills exhibited by the young boy, and persuaded good friend Wayne Meyer to watch him play. Director of player personnel for the Western Hockey League's Portland Winterhawks, Meyer made the journey from Oregon to see John in action. He liked what he saw, and promptly placed the hulking hockey player on the list of players invited to the 1982-83 Winterhawks' training camp, to be held in nearby Red Deer. Kozak met with the Kordics, and convinced them to have their son sign a major junior contract with Portland. To seal the deal, Meyer promised that John's education would be fully paid for.

Kordic flew to Oregon in July, where he signed a contract and received a new team jacket. Upon his son's return, Ivan registered him at the Tomohawk Hockey School, where young John held his own against the likes of WHL stars Rob Brown and Greg Hawgood. At the Winterhawks' camp in the fall, he soon befriended future NHL star Cam Neely, and made friends with resident tough-guy defenseman Kelly Hubbarb, who gladly taught John how to fight effectively. Towards the end of camp, Kordic was delighted to find out that he had made the club.

ENFORCER IN JUNIOR HOCKEY

Defending WHL champs, Portland had captured the Western Division in three of the past four seasons. Owner Brian Shaw had decided four years earlier to move the struggling franchise from Edmonton to the U.S. state of Oregon; the relocation met with great success, and attendance at Memorial Coliseum was always near-capacity for home games.

Kordic fit right in with the club, his fighting prowess quickly winning over local fans. In the season opener he pummeled into submission tough guy Jamie Crayford, in the process displaying the grace and style of a pro boxer and using his ambidexterity to land thundering left- and right-handed hooks with equal ease. Portland fans claimed they had never seen anyone fight that well, and within weeks John had established himself as the team's best defenseman and the league's most feared warrior. Kordic's parents went to many of the games and did not approve of their son's fighting; they evened stormed out of the arena in a huff one night, when John badly beat up Seattle enforcer Scott Walker. When their son came to the hotel later that night to visit, an irate Ivan slammed the door in his face.[3]

The powerhouse Winterhawks led the Western Division for most of the regular campaign, but as the playoffs neared Kordic found himself in the doghouse of the coach, Ken Hodge; his power-play time and role as top defenseman had been taken away. Despite the team's on-ice success, widespread rumors of steroid use by the players dogged the franchise. Former Portland star Gary Nylund, then just starting his NHL career, charged that players were often forced to fight opponents hopped-up on steroids, but the accusations went unproven. Kordic himself candidly admitted that some teammates abused alcohol and marijuana, yet those allegations eventually died down. In the playoffs the Winterhawks beat Victoria in the Division championships, advancing to the WHL finals against the Lethbridge Broncos.

The Broncos won, but both teams advanced to the prestigious Memorial Cup. John and his parents continually pleaded with coach Hodge to give him more ice time, aware that NHL scouts were in the stands. Portland defeated the Oshawa Generals to capture the title, but it was a bitter-sweet campaign for infrequently used Kordic.

In the 1983-84 season Portland owner Brian Shaw responded to allegations of drug abuse on the club by establishing hockey's first drug program.

On the ice the Winterhawks started strong, posting a 10-2 record, but then slumped badly. Kordic did not have a good campaign, his aggressiveness often leading to foolish penalties, his rushes up ice with the puck often resulting in giveaways and goals against. Hodge liked the fact that John played hard, but wanted him to play smarter. Finishing at 33-39, Portland barely made the playoffs, but advanced to face New Westminister in the Division finals. In game six, with his team leading the series 3-2, Kordic played his best game as a Winterhawks. John blocked shots with reckless abandon, made big and timely hits, cleared the defensive zone effectively, and handled the puck with authority. Portland won the game and series, advancing to the WHL finals against the mighty Kamloops Blazers, who then swept past the Winterhawks.

The 1984 NHL Entry Draft was held in Montreal that summer, but the once personable defenseman was now being widely perceived as a risky selection, in light of his strained relationship with Hodge, his moody personality, and his bad season. Ivan Kordic promised a big family celebration, having anticipated John being chosen in the first round, but his son was not chosen until the fourth round, by the Montreal Canadiens.

Elated at being taken by the legendary Habs, Kordic was enthusiastic at the team's training camp, but he knew realistically he would probably end up back in junior. Dell Wilson, the club's chief western scout, advised him to work hard, stay focused, and avoid the city's late night temptations. General Manager Serge Savard and the rookie coach Jean Perron both hoped that Kordic would fill Chris Nilan's enforcer role when the latter retired, and were initially impressed with his aggressiveness. Management took note of the decisive manner in which the young player bested heavyweight Murray Baron during a scrimmage game fight, soon after dispatching him back to junior so that he could further develop his playing skills.

The Winterhawks welcomed Kordic back into the fray, aware that most of its marquee players had moved on to the NHL or AHL. John was voted team captain, but was an impatient and temperamental leader, harshly criticizing younger teammates as the team struggled early in the season. Kordic himself neglected his defensive duties to often launch solo, futile forays up ice.

Bothered by John's negative attitude at practice, and reports he was breaking curfew, Hodge benched him by November.

Many familiar with the uneasy situation feel, in hindsight, that John's surly attitude may have resulted from sexual abuse at the hands of owner Brian Shaw, who once allegedly confessed that he "liked what he saw (of Kordic on the ice), but he really liked what he saw in the shower."[4] After Shaw's death from AIDS-related cancer in 1993, there were rumors that he had sexual relations with young players, but these remain unproven. John had allegedly hinted that he was abused at the hands of Shaw, but nothing came of it.

Although Kordic had 25 points in 31 games for the WinterHawks, in December Hodge arranged a trade which would have sent the enforcer to the Brandon Wheat Kings. John refused to go, eventually accepting a deal to Seattle, where his offensive capabilities and fighting skills made him an instant fan favorite. Picking up 17 goals and 36 assists, he finished his final WHL season with 78 points, his best ever, and was chosen to the league's Second All-Star Team, behind first team defensemen Glen Wesley and Wendel Clark.

At the end of the WHL season, John was transferred to Montreal's American Hockey League farm club, the Sherbrooke Canadiens, to add toughness to the talented team's late-season playoff drive. Sherbrooke's on-ice play was suffering since it lacked a tough guy to make sure opponents did not take advantage of softer, skilled players, future Montreal stars like Stephane Richer, Claude Lemieux, Mike Keane, and Patrick Roy. Kordic promptly served notice, beating up heavyweights Val James of St. Catherines and Torrie Robertson of Binghampton. The AHL club displayed a new sense of confidence with John in its line-up, winning 27 of its final 34 games to squeak into the playoffs, then capping off an improbable run by edging Baltimore for the AHL's Calder Cup title.

STANLEY CUP GLORY

Kordic played five regular season games for the Montreal Canadiens in 1985-86, but spent most of the year with Sherbrooke, often terrorizing meeker opponents and firmly entrenching himself as the AHL's most feared heavyweight. He was recalled by Montreal on the eve of the 1986 Stanley Cup playoffs, to provide a physical presence in the tougher post-season games.

Summoning John to his office, coach Perron asked him to protect the team's smaller, skilled players but to avoid needless penalties or dropping the gloves just for the sake of it.[5] He was also told he would be playing right wing as opposed to defense, where his limited lateral movement might cause problems for the Habs.

Having finished second in the rugged Adams Divsion, Montreal faced the Boston Bruins in the opening round. Perron wanted tough forward Chris Nilan to focus on playing hockey, and newcomer Kordic to handle any fighting which was required; the coach was concerned that Nilan, an emotional native Bostonian, would be goaded into unnecessary battles. The strategy worked; Nilan played well and contributed points, Kordic laid a beating on Bruins' tough guy Jay Miller, and the Habs swept the series. John's unanimous decision over Miller earned him the nickname Rambo.

The Canadiens then defeated the Hartford Whalers to win the Adams Division title, advancing to the Eastern Conference finals against the New York Rangers. Montreal beat the Rangers to advance to the Stanley Cup finals against the Calgary Flames, but the most memorable series incident came when Kordic badly bloodied New York's heavyweight George McPhee.[6] Hovering triumphantly over his fallen opponent, John then kissed his fists as he skated away; this pompous behavior would become his trademark whenever he bested another tough guy.[7]

Kordic was used sparingly in the Cup finals, a relatively tame affair, but he did best Calgary's Tim Hunter in another bloodfest. Leading the series 3-2 in games, the Halos then defeated the Flames at the Calgary Saddledome to capture the Cup, and rookie goalie Patrick Roy won the Conn Smythe Trophy as the Most Valuable Player.

After the game, champagne flowed freely in the Canadiens' dressing room, as the players savored their hard-fought victory. Embracing his father Ivan, Kordic was never happier. "I'm the luckiest guy on earth," he exclaimed to The Edmonton Journal. "First the Memorial Cup, then the Calder Cup, now the Stanley Cup. I think I'll go out and play the lottery next."[8]

The Canadiens signed their enforcer to a three-year contract at $150,000 annually before he returned to Edmonton for the summer, soon starting to date Sandy Bernard, an attractive local woman. Attending Church regularly and going out with Sandy and his friends in the evenings, he also was a guest instructor at local hockey schools and started a personal body-building program.

Rumors circulated that he was taking steroids, and former childhood coach Bill Laforge feared the worst one day, when he noticed John's rippling muscles and the strange prescription bottles in his gym bag. Confronting his former player, Laforge was bluntly told that one had to maintain body strength to successfully compete in the NHL.[9]

TROUBLED ROOKIE IN MONTREAL

Kordic was still technically a rookie when he arrived at the Habs' 1986-87 training camp, but his new muscled physique made him less mobile and not nearly as effective as he had been the past spring. Well aware of rumors of John's cocaine use, Perron was now concerned he was using steroids. "I couldn't believe it," the former Montreal coach recalled. "How could you bulk yourself up the way he did? He was all bulked up, I mean four months earlier he was playing at a weight of 205 and then all of a sudden he's playing at 225...I got phone calls saying he was on steroids and people were asking me to look after him."[10] Kordic had lost his position on the fourth line by the time the regular campaign started, and the enforcer settled into the role of fringe player, seldom seeing quality ice time.

John and some of his teammates started hanging out at bars and strip clubs on Crescent Street early in the season, and a story circulated that Kordic has snorted cocaine with a well-known organized-crime figure in an Italian district bar named Larmac II (The Sting), where underworld mobsters often gathered. Owned by the enforcer's friend Michel Labonte, a local competitive kick-boxer, the bar was eventually declared off limits by Habs management. When the rookie contracted a sexually-transmitted disease, Perron had the team trainers purify the dressing room whirlpool.

Not playing much and in poor shape in spite of his strength, Kordic was sent to Sherbrooke for reconditioning at mid-season. When he was recalled two weeks later, he was fighting even more. After a violent outburst in the coach's office over his lack of playing time, John was reprimanded after complaining to the press about being mismanaged. The local press tagged him with the moniker The Incredible Hulk; some reporters claimed that he threatened to harm Perron and his family.

The coach soon became more worried about Kordic's strained relationship with his father. John often had shouting matches on the phone with his dad, who adamantly voiced disapproval of the fighting and violence. "How many times did I see John Kordic crying into a phone after a game that we won," Perron asked. "I would say, `John, we won the game! What's the problem, and he would say, my father watched the game. I fought, he does not accept it, and I do not know what to do. I would say, `John, you have a job in the NHL but if you improve your skills you will get more ice time and maybe fighting will become a second asset in your career.'"[11]

The irony, of course, was that Kordic needed more ice time to develop his game, but that was not forthcoming in Montreal. "He hated fighting," Toni Kordic, his sister, asserted, "but he felt he had to in order to keep his job."[12] Perron noted, however, a contradiction with the enforcer. "He said he didn't want to fight, but he actually loved to fight," he claimed. "He loved the attention and the only way for him to attract attention was to fight."[13]

In 44 games, John managed just five goals and 8 points but accumulated 151 penalty minutes. Just before season's end Perron received a letter from Kordic's parents which discussed their son's battle with cocaine. The letter asked the Montreal coach to watch over him. On the ice, Kordic saw little action in the playoffs as the second-place Canadiens advanced to the Eastern Conference finals, where the club promptly lost to the Philadelphia Flyers.

PROBLEMS IN QUEBEC

Kordic had lost the respect of many teammates by the start of his second season. They accepted his devotion to the enforcer role, but wanted to distance themselves from his controversial lifestyle. The Canadiens started out strong, leading the division for most of the year, but again Kordic hardly played. He became a loner off the ice. Some nights John stayed home alone, surfing the movie channels on his big screen TV; other evenings he went out alone, frequenting seedy strip joints in the city's north end.[14] He found time to model in photo-shoots for Bitterman Leather Apparel and Bauer Skates.

In February, Kordic fought Quebec enforcer Gord Donnelly in a much-publicized, pre-game bout. The NHL promptly fined both teams $25,000 and their coaches $1000 each, arguing that Perron and Ron Lapointe of the Nordiques had encouraged the fight to hype their teams' rivalry. In his defense, Perron blamed the combatants themselves, and the two players were suspended for five games.

Later in the year, the embattled Montreal coach was angrily confronted by Canadiens winger Claude Lemieux in an unrelated incident, but John displayed his loyalty to Perron by promptly roughing up Lemieux. The team was in turmoil, but still finished first in the Adams; Kordic's ice time was sporadic, and he ended up with two goals and 159 penalty minutes in 60 games. He hardly played in the post-season, as the Habs advanced to the division finals, where they lost to Boston.

Perron's relationship with several of his players had proved very controversial, and in the off-season he was fired. The replacement was the late Pat Burns, a former Ontario policeman and noted disciplinarian. Relations between Kordic and Burns were predictably frosty at the 1988-89 training camp, and around this time the ex-cop might have used his professional contacts to confirm the winger's problems with booze, cocaine, and strippers. Invariably the last man on the ice and the first one off at practice, his bad attitude kept him out of any pre-season games. Kordic's poor fitness was evident when Burns tried to slip him into the line-up early in the regular campaign, and was further angered when the enforcer continued to be late for practice. Kordic's friend Michel Labonte and Molstar exec Poulin Tardiff, who had taken the forward in as a border that summer, were also concerned when he disappeared for a few days or displayed irrational bouts of paranoia.

In early November, having played only four games with no points and thirteen penalty minutes, John got into an explosive confrontation with Burns over his lack of ice time, the exchange almost coming to blows. The former Habs' coach later empathized with the troubled player. "It's difficult to keep up the tough guy image," Burns asserted, "and if you don't, people don't want you around anymore."[15] Nevertheless, General Manager Savard started shopping the troubled enforcer around the league, and on November 8th traded Kordic and a sixth round draft choice to the Toronto Maple Leafs for offensive forward Russ Courtnall. Aware that any discussion of Kordic's drug problems might get him suspended for life under the league's zero-tolerance policy, Savard told the press that his lack of ice time was the main reason for the trade.

TURBULENCE IN TORONTO

Convinced he would be going to the Edmonton Oilers, who had expressed interest, Kordic was disappointed to be heading to Toronto. A proud franchise with a winning tradition, the Maple Leafs had deteriorated significantly under the destructive, meddling ownership of Harold Ballard. Ballard and then-coach John Brophy, a former tough-guy in the old East Coast League, prodded 30-year-old General Manager Gord Stellick into trading for Kordic to add toughness to the club. Information did not travel well in the stagnant organization, however, and Stellick was unaware of Kordic's drug habits, despite hearing rumors of his fast lifestyle.[16]

Accustomed to being treated more like a star in Montreal, John was labelled a goon by the Toronto press, which lamented the trading of the skilled Courtnall. Kordic was disappointed that the Leafs players did not enjoy commercial endorsements available in Montreal, and lampooned their poor weight-lifting and training equipment. Already in last place in the Norris Divsion, the sad-sack Leafs continued to lose, and Brophy would often send Kordic onto the ice to stir things up late in the game.

On December 10th, he was suspended ten games for breaking Keith Acton's nose. During that time, Toronto police tipped off the team's management that undercover cops had witnessed John downtown, getting involved with drugs and prostitutes. Confronted by Stellick, Kordic explained that he was just trying to make new friends in the city, but teammates kept their distance from him, nicknaming him sniffy, in reference to his alleged cocaine use. Stories surfaced that John was buying coke and the services of hookers from two brothers originally from Edmonton, who were pimping in Toronto.[17]

Former Leaf captain George Armstrong had reluctantly replaced Brophy behind the bench in late December, and soon grew tired of Kordic's antics, frequently benching him. With the Leafs set to play in Montreal near the end of the season, John looked forward to playing against his former teammates, but was benched for the game. Embarrassed, he argued with Armstrong on the bench, then stormed off to the dressing room as the game ended. He later was alleged to have disciplined former Leaf Gary Leeman, after the latter was said to be having an affair with a teammate's wife.[18]

In a season split between the Habs and the Leafs, he netted one goal in 52 games to go with 198 penalty minutes, and the moribund Leafs finished with a 28-46-8 record, last in the Norris Division and out of the playoffs. On the plane trip home after the last game, a loss to Chicago, the Leaf coaches and players looked on nervously as the enraged hockey player openly vented his anger and frustration. Already disturbed, Kordic then learned that his father was dying of cancer when he got to Toronto.

Returning to Alberta to visit his sick father and see his girlfriend Sandy, the couple was drinking in a bar called Barry T's one night, when she was verbally assaulted by two guys who had tried to pick her up. Kordic almost fought both men, but Ken Lacusta, the Canadian Heavyweight Boxing Champion, stepped in. After harsh words, Lacusta and Kordic took their ensuing argument to the parking lot, where the two warriors stared each other down before deciding not to tussle.[19]

THE DOWNWARD SPIRAL

Kordic was distraught when his father died just prior to the start of 1989-90, having never achieved any sense of closure in their troubled relationship. Feeling that he let his dad down by using his fighting rather than playing skills, John had lost all self-respect. With Ivan having passed on, he sank into a deeper funk, and began abusing drugs and alcohol more than ever. He smashed his red Corvette sportscar twice in the ensuing months, began skipping practices and games without permission, and hung out with the wrong crowd late into the night.

The Maple Leaf enforcer candidly discussed his predicament after a practice early in the season. "In the beginning it didn't bother me so much but in the end it starts to bother you," he admitted. "You want to play and you want to contribute more than fisticuffs and stuff like that. But they say everyone has a role and you have to accept it and that's been the tough part for me right now...to accept my role."[20]

The Leafs were a stronger team, largely due to the stability that new coach Doug Carpenter brought to the embattled club. Carpenter encouraged John to speak his mind, and asked assistant coaches Mike Kitchen and Gary Lariviere to watch over the troubled player. Playing regularly and even seeing some power-play time, Kordic responded by playing decent hockey, but was soon battling old demons. Management grew suspicious of his chronic money problems, and at least twice he asked for a salary advance.

While his witty one-liners ingratiated him to teammates, most kept their distance. After a fight, he would often go directly to the Leafs' dressing room even though he was not injured in the tussle. Captain Rob Ramage criticized him in the press for his bad attitude and work habits and the team soon suspended him without pay, but attempts to trade him at the March deadline proved futile.

When Regina Kordic flew in from Edmonton and visited her son late in the season, John's attitude improved somewhat. Still unofficially suspended, he was allowed to practice with the team again.[21] In spite of all the personal turmoil, Kordic played in 55 games, notching a career-high 9 goals, 13 points, and 252 penalty minutes. Toronto posted a respectable 38-38-4 record and 80 points, the most by a Leaf team in eleven years. Finishing third in the Norris Division, the club still lost its opening playoff round. Kordic returned to Edmonton in the off-season, moving in with Sandy and frequenting the downtown bars. Toronto arranged for John to attend Henwood, an alcohol and drug rehabilitation center, but he was soon asked to leave after heated confrontations with other patients.[22]

The Leafs promptly issued an ultimatum to clean up his act, and in June he checked into Sierra Tuscon, a highly respected substance abuse facility in Arizona. Counselors and psychologists conducted in-depth interviews with John, during which he admitting using alcohol by the age of 13, cocaine by the age of 23, and steroids for the past three NHL seasons. He also conceded that he had spent over $80,000 in cocaine, and often experienced such symptoms as "easy fatigability shortness of breath, sweating, cold hands, dizziness, light-headedness, trouble falling asleep and staying awake, dry mouth, difficulty concentrating, feeling keyed up and on edge."[23]

The experts at Sierra Tuscon related his moody depressions and destructive behavior to problems in his personal relationships, particularly unresolved issues with his deceased father. Kordic soon wore out his welcome when confronted by other patients and staff for his breaches of in-patient conduct codes and patient confidentiality; he was alleged to have searched through the personal files of a female patient and to have joked about blackmailing her over something in her past. Before discharging him, the facility recommended that he undergo more re-hab and a twelve-step program, but admitted that his prognosis for success was poor.[24]

Kordic showed up at the Leafs' 1990 training camp with a bad attitude, soon being arrested for assault after a scuffle in a bar, in which he broke his cell phone over the head of a young man. A few nights later, TV cameras filmed John in a private box during an exhibition match at the Gardens, drinking alcohol and cheering against the Leafs. Demoted to the AHL's Newmarket Saints, he responded to tough coach Frank Anzalone, soon embracing his enforcer role and even scoring a game-winner against Maine. Within a month, however, Kordic had reverted back to his old ways, fighting with a teammate on the bench, and spitting at a referee. Eventually he was suspended by the league for vulgar gestures directed at hostile fans of the Capital District Islanders. Anzalone was very disappointed, and Maple Leaf General Manager Floyd Smith, having long since given the tough guy's No. 27 jersey to Lucien Deblois, forbade Kordic from practising with the Saints. In late January the Leafs dealt Kordic and Paul Fenton to the Washington Capitals for future considerations.

CHANCE WITH THE CAPS

Well aware of Kordic's bad reputation, Washington's General Manager David Poile still felt that he could add much-needed toughness to the soft, struggling Capitals club. "One wrong move and John's out of here in a second," he told the press. "We're taking a small risk in terms of what we're giving up to get John…but let's be honest, if we were in first place right now rather than fifth, we'd never have made the deal. He's very definitely a man on the bubble."[25]

In his very first game, Kordic fought New York Islander tough guy Mitch Vukota, and then racked up a lot of penalty minutes in a fight-filled match against the Flyers. His tough play helped the Capitals go 4-0-1, but he frequently missed practices. After one occasion, Capitals' defenseman Mike Lalor, a former Habs teammate, visited Kordic's residence, but the paranoid enforcer refused to let him in for fifteen minutes, muttering "this isn't my place, this isn't my apartment."

Another relapse landed him in Alcoholics Anonymous, but his teammates displayed a show of confidence by voting him back into the line-up for an upcoming game against the Rangers. He was suspended by the team after a third re-lapse, and watched the game from the pressbox. "It's a day-to-day thing...Today, I've beaten it today, but I haven't beaten it today. I haven't gone to bed yet," he conceded. "We tied a game here, 4-4. The guys are going to want to go out and have a bite to eat and a few drinks... It's a daily thing, it's a daily battle and tomorrow's another day and another battle."[26]

Sent to the famous Hazeldon Clinic in Minnesota, a health facility for chemical dependents, Kordic was placed under the care of renowned drug therapist Dr. James Fearing. He was moved to a half-way house at the end of May after experiencing trouble opening up in group therapy sessions. Befriended by former North Star coach Glen Sonmor, a recovering alcoholic who took him to AA meetings, John also became buddies with Nordiques' defenseman Bryan Fogarty, also in re-hab at a nearby half-way house.

He also allegedly sneaked out with another player in the middle of night to drink, and he left the city before the program ended, thereby aborting any hopes of returning to the Capitals. With no points and 101 penalty minutes in his brief tour with Washington, he returned to Montreal in July, coming to the aid of Michel Labonte's teenage son later that summer, when the boy was reportedly swarmed by a group of young men.[27]

LES NORDIQUES ENTER THE PICTURE

Quebec General Manager Pierre Page needed a marquee player to help put fans in the Coliseum seats in 1991-92, having lost sniper Valeri Kamensky to injury and junior star Eric Lindros to Philadelphia. After Fogarty recommended Kordic, even offering to room with him, the Nordiques executive met with the enforcer and offered an unusual contract: $1500 for each game he played, $1000 if he did not play, and $150,000 at the end of the regular season if he passed random urine tests throughout the regular campaign. Quebec could terminate the deal at any time.

The Nordiques arranged to help John sort out his financial situation early in the season, and with Kordic wearing No. 43 to Forgarty's No. 44 jersey, the enforcer seemed content. When the hulking 235-pounder hit the ice Quebec fans routinely chanted Kord-ique! Kord-ique! Fogarty and Kordic were seen in public, nursing soft drinks; John made a sincere attempt to go straight. "(In rehab) we were told to think what's going to happen if you have that one drink," he confessed alongside Fogarty in a local TV news interview. "And you think, well, one's going to turn into two, two's going to turn into four, who knows if I'm going to be out of a job again, I'll be hanging out with these bums again... It's just things I don't want to start doing all over again."[28] John later moved in with Nancy Masse, a Quebec City stripper.

Kordic suffered another re-lapse early on, when the Nordiques were in Montreal. His aberrant and volatile late-night behavior in the Sheraton Hotel, where the team was staying, so alarmed Page that he promptly had the burly winger tested for drugs, and sat him for the game against the Canadiens. Relations between the enforcer and Fogarty also worsened, as the latter tried to stay clean.

John was allowed to return to the team when the test came back slightly positive but inconclusive. Results did not indicate either drugs or alcohol in his system, but hinted at steroids. In fact, his chiseled physique resembled that of a heavy steroid user, and by November he was actually cycling different pills in 6-to-8 week periods, soon graduating to more exotic steroids, which were injected though the buttocks. This required larger needles and syringes, which Kordic detested.[29]

Kordic had a strained relationship with his brother, Dan, then just a rookie with the rugged Flyers. "That little shit, I'm going to kick his ass," he told Nancy one night, "He thinks he's better than me."[30] Dressing for a game against Philadelphia in December, he exchanged harsh words with Dan before the opening face-off. "I asked Dan if he had spent any time with John and he said, 'nope, just said hello to him this morning,'" a sports announcer said during before the TV broadcast of that game, "so apparently they are not very close."[31] When the puck dropped, Kordic went at it with tough guy Dave Brown. It was one of his last hockey fights.

Page soon met with Kordic's increasingly concerned family, and started leaving the enforcer in Quebec City during the Nordiques' road trips. Nancy had to rescue her hopped-up boyfriend one night at the Hotel Pierre, and was very worried by the depressed hockey player's fatalistic words. "All my life I wanted to make my father proud - it's like I can feel him inside me. I don't know anymore, maybe if I was dead I'd be closer to him, maybe I deserve to be dead," he confided to her. "My dad was my idol and when he died I was mad at myself. I never said the things I should have said. My whole career, I did it against his will. I'm not going to live to be his age. I'm not going to make it to forty."[32]

When another drug test came pack positive in late January, Page informed Kordic that he had been voted off the team, and said that he would die if he did not get help. The troubled winger's tour with Quebec was done after only 19 games; he had tallied just two assists and 115 penalty minutes. No mention of alcohol or drugs was made when the Nords' executives informed the press that John had been released.

CAPE BRETON: END OF THE ROAD

Edmonton signed John to a minor-league contract for the rest of the season. Reporting to their farm club, the AHL's Cape Breton Oilers, he was anxious to prove himself and get called up to the NHL club. Perhaps he knew it was his last chance in pro hockey. Kordic curtailed his drinking and started an intense weight-training program, and the muscular forward played on a makeshift fourth line with fellow heavyweight Louie Debrusk. Kordic's added toughness helped the club go on a ten-game winning streak, earning the grudging respect of his meeker teammates. Other squads became leery of playing the Oilers, and the enforcer was known to taunt opponents during the morning skate by sternly warning them that you can run, but you can't hide!

John roomed with Debrusk, himself a recovering alcoholic, and two men soon became friends. On several occasions Louie and other Oilers witnessed

Kordic inject steroids before a game, and John told them he wasn't afraid to die.[33] Continuing his steroid recycling program, Kordic mostly kept to himself in Nova Scotia, often telephoning Nancy or his agent, whom he pestered about being called up to Edmonton. John allegedly called Oilers' General Manager Glen Sather a liar, claiming that Sather broke a promise to bring him up for the Stanley Cup playoffs.[34] After Cape Breton was ousted from the AHL post-season, Kordic returned to Quebec City for the summer.

A WILD AND FATAL RIDE

John was ecstatic to learn that Nancy was pregnant. The couple became engaged soon after, but she was reluctant to have the baby if he could not get clean. Desperate to recapture an enforcer role with an NHL team, Kordic continued to ingest steroids and weight-lift heavily. By now his intense steroid use left the hulking, 235-pounder subject to frequent steroid-induced rages, as well as heavy perspiring and breathing. Nancy later recalled bouts of euphoria and black depression. He made several cash withdrawals on a $16,000 cheque from the Nordiques he had deposited.

The beginning of the end came in early August, when Kordic was arrested over a domestic dispute involving Nancy and her former boyfriend. Upon his release the next day, he was told to stay away from her for a period of ten days, although Nancy had merely wanted him out of the house for the night.

For the next few days John moved from hotel to hotel. On August 8th at around 3 a.m., he hailed a taxi and drove to the Motel Maxim; with Kordic breathing and sweating profusely, the cab driver stopped at a convenience store so the hockey player could pick up a large bottle of Pepsi, which he thirstily gulped down. After a very brief stay at the motel, the restless player took a second cab to the Hotel Luxembourg.

Checking out of the hotel around 8 a.m., John hailed yet another taxi, and drove around the city for hours; the driver noticed John was in obvious pain, often slamming his large fists against his head, as if he had a severe migraine. After checking in at the Hotel Luxembourg again, he repeatedly phoned the lobby receptionist throughout the day, asking where he was and who he was, obviously confused and disoriented.

A hotel employee delivered beer to Kordic's hotel room around 3 p.m., and saw blood on the enforcer's hands and all over the carpet, drapes and furniture. John left the hotel around 5 p.m, but it was not until the next day that housekeeping would find the room in a shambles, with broken furniture tossed about, a giant hole in the ceiling, and small and large bloodstains everywhere.

John returned to the Hotel Maxim around 6 p.m., and his behavior turned more bizarre as the evening progressed; loud banging noises emanated from his hotel room, and his strange telephone calls continually harassed front desk personnel. Hotel director Serge Bouchard finally called L'Ancienne Lorette Police Station at 9:30 p.m., and about half an hour later police converged on the hotel. Also summoned was the Quebec Provincial Police, but officers were instructed to remove their weapons before entering Kordic's hotel room.

Seven police officers entered the room around 10:04 p.m., and their efforts to subdue the enraged hockey player soon spun out of control. In a blind rage, probably induced by the massive intake of drugs, the burly Kordic repeatedly charged at the policemen, like an angry bull or determined linebacker. Perhaps using excessive force, the police pinned Kordic's back, arms and legs to the floor, crowding him to the point where he could not breathe. They called for an ambulance when John began frothing at the mouth, the first signs of cardiac arrest.

By the time the ambulance personnel arrived, Kordic's face was flush red, and his stiff, blue body made no sounds as it was lifted onto the stretcher. In all the commotion, ambulance attendant Mario Desrosiers witnessed one policeman brazenly kneeling on the back of the stricken hockey player, posing as if he had just bagged a lion on a Safari hunt.

Attendants were unable to revive Kordic in the speeding ambulance, and his pulse and respiration were extremely weak when the vehicle arrived at the University Hospital du Laval around 11 p.m. Hospital workers then waited over ten minutes before finally providing John with much needed oxygen, but by then it was too late. He died around 11:11 p.m., officially pronounced dead by Dr. Deschaine at 11:41 p.m.

The evidence collected by police from John's hotel room at the Hotel Maxim had indicated heavy drug use as the major cause of death: three used syringes, a box of unused needles, an empty bottle of Stern (an exotic blend of three steroids), and bottles containing common steroids such as Muscle Flex, Uni Test Suspension, Baldone, and Winstrol V. Shattered glass and broken furniture was evidence of the violent struggle which had taken place between Kordic and the police.

An autopsy was performed at the hospital on Kordic's body the next day by Dr. George Miller. Consistent with steroid use, Kordic was found to have an enlarged spleen, an enlarged liver and lungs three times their normal size. In his written report, Miller concluded the cause of death as "arrhythmic cardiac arrest followed by violent effort under the influence of cocaine, severe pulmonary edema, and aspirations of bronchitis, and food substances in the lungs".

"A WALKING TIME BOMB" – REACTION TO KORDIC'S DEATH

Many NHL players and management were not surprised by Kordic's death. "It's like John had a time bomb inside him," said Pierre Page, "a time bomb set to explode."[35] Former Leafs General Manager Gord Stellick agreed. "I talked to him once or twice, but I was gone (as Leafs GM) by the time he really started getting into trouble. He was a walking time bomb that was getting ready to explode."[36] Stellick felt that it was only a matter of time before Kordic met with tragedy. "I really didn't expect it to be this soon, but it really was inevitable," he asserted. "I saw him throw not just his career away but his life. I really liked the guy. There was a good side to him but it was obvious he was into something bad. But he'd just lie to you about it."[37]

Pierre Beauchemin, then the Nordiques team physician, discussed Kordic's regular use of steroids. "Everyone knows that steroids can enhance the aggressiveness, the temper, the sexual drive," he said, "For people who are already aggressive human beings, steroids can put them over the edge."[38] John's former roommate in Quebec, Bruce Cashman, argued that the cocaine was responsible for the tragedy. "He must have been on a very bad trip.

When he was doing cocaine he would become very, very paranoid," Cashman said. "When he saw all those policemen there, he must have gone crazy." Told that police did not find any cocaine in the room, Cashman replied "that is probably because he (Kordic) took it all."[39] Nancy Masse noted that John was claustrophobic and scared of the police. "When he was handcuffed and thrown into the back of an ambulance, with cops all around, his heart couldn't take it," she said. "No one deserves to die that way."[40]

Former Leaf Jim McKenny, himself an admitted former cocaine user, concurred. "Low self-esteem, then the drugs," McKenny said, referring to possible triggers that set Kordic off. "All the drugs are linked. A guy like him will have two or three drinks, then he wants to get into the blow, then to take the edge off he has five or six drinks to get level again, then he'll get pumped up on steroids and start all over again. It sounds crazy, but to him it was a way of life."[41]

When John Brophy heard about John's death, he could not help thinking about Ivan Kordic. "I think when his father died it really messed him up. His father had some control over him but once he died, that was gone," Brophy figured. "He couldn't handle either success or failure, I guess. He was a tough kid, physically, he was very tough. But I coached him with Montreal's farm team and from the time I had him he was a high-strung kid, but not in a bad way."[42] The veteran coach later expressed guilt over John's demise. "It doesn't matter now but I'll take the blame for it. I noticed a change in the kid when he came to Toronto," Brophy said. "I thought he had done an excellent job for the Canadiens. In Toronto he was only fair. I thought the death of his dad might have had something to do with it. They were always close."[43]

Toronto sportswriter Damien Cox recalled when he met with Kordic, who had recently been suspended by the Leafs. Kordic lamented over his inability to stay out of trouble, talked of an unsuccessful suicide attempt the previous season, and worried about whether fans accepted him. "I guess I've just taken everything for granted," he told Cox, as he cried. "I just can't believe I let it go this far. I never realized things were this bad."[44]

Aside from his personal troubles and his tragic demise, Kordic the player was also remembered, even with regret. "He could play," Regina Kordic declared of her son. "But something went wrong. He started using his fists.

After awhile, I didn't recognize my kid. I didn't raise him that way."[45] Perron remembered how his fighting abilities made him the toast of Montreal. "He beat the shit out of everybody. He was the best fighter in the league. Nobody could take John Kordic. The fans in the Forum would chant his name, Kor-dic! Kor-dic! Kor-dic," Perron later said. "After he beat up Gord Donnelly of the Nordiques before an opening face-off in Quebec (1988), as he was skating off the ice he kissed his fist and held it up to the crowd. I never saw anyone else do that, before or since."[46]

Stellick also discussed how Kordic's fighting abilities made him enormously popular with the fans. He recalled how he received one of the loudest ovations on the opening night of the 1989-90 season. "I remember thinking, if he can only keep it together," Stellick reflected. "I couldn't have been more wrong."[47] Former Leafs teammate Brad Marsh recalled a talent wasted. "I think about sitting next to him in the dressing room and thinking about how many people would have given their right arm to have a piece of what he had," March remembered. "There was always so much promise to John Kordic. Now we'll never know."[48]

Funeral services for Kordic were held at a Croatian church in Edmonton a few days after his death. Attended by over 400 people, services commenced with a moving sermon by Father Cunningham. Kordic's body was later laid to rest at St. Albert's Cemetery, next to his late father's.

MEDIA COVERAGE SPARKS PUBLIC INQUIRY

Intense media coverage in the aftermath of Kordic's death made the public aware of the circumstances surrounding his demise and eventually sparked a public inquiry in Quebec; it also helped compel the NHL to revise its substance abuse policies. On August 24th Sports Illustrated magazine published a controversial article entitled "Death of a Goon", alleging that drug use might be widespread in pro hockey. In one particular instance the article quoted Bruce Cashman on John's drug problems. "John wasn't an alcoholic. He drank, yes, but only when he did drugs.

He was a drug addict," Cashman asserted. "He was addicted to cocaine and had been since he played for Montreal. He said it was a big thing with the Canadiens. John said a coach walked into the hotel room where a couple of players were doing drugs, and the coach just said, 'I didn't see that' and turned around and walked out the door."[49] This stunning allegation was supported by Nancy Masse. "John told me he was doing coke with another player when a coach came in," she said. "The coach didn't say anything. He just walked away."[50]

That same day another article, entitled "Death of an Enforcer", happened to be published in The Western Report. In it Kordic's childhood coach Bill Laforge said that John's problems with steroids started in Portland, when management pressured him into fighting.[51] The WHL later asked the weekly publication to retract the story, but Lillian Kordic, John's sister, later wrote Laforge a letter, congratulating him on the courage to tell the truth.

Media coverage of the Kordic saga started to fade across Canada by the fall, but not so in Quebec. Radio talk-show host Andres Arturs bluntly asserted that John's death was largely the result of police brutality, and former Habs coach Jean Perron discussed the incident at length on his popular talk radio show, alluding to widespread substance abuse in the NHL. Such press compelled Quebec's provincial government to act. On October 7th, Chief Coroner Jean Grenier ordered a formal public inquiry into Kordic's death. Soon after, the Quebec Provincial Police launched its own internal investigation of the involvement of its officers in the incident.

THE PUBLIC INQUIRY IS LAUNCHED

Lasting over seven months, the public inquiry considered 61 items of evidence, and heard testimony from over 60 people. It was supervised by coroner Gerald Lucas and concluded April 26, 1993. The primary finding was that hockey player John Kordic died form a lethal amount of cocaine, and that this process was somewhat exacerbated by police intervention. The inquiry also asserted, however, that the actions of the police were justified in light of Kordic's resistance and the limited training methods available to them at the time. Ambulance personnel were found to have been relatively slow, and their knowledge of proper procedures limited.[52]

Forensic toxicologists found a lethal cocaine concentration of 0.13 mg per 100 g of blood in his system, coupled with his agitated condition, this gave him a dire need for oxygen. "Not only was he not able to get the oxygen he needed, but pressure put on his back by the policemen... stopped him from breathing properly," Lucas deduced from his findings. "The same result occurred when they tied his hands behind his back. This put pressure on his chest...his heart became more contracted and the blood did not circulate well – flowing in another direction towards his lungs to promote the pulmonary edema which brought the asphyxia that caused the death."[53]

Police testimony at the inquiry had alluded to appropriate behavior by the officers involved, but Lucas was critical of one of the superior officers, named Janvier, who had allegedly struck the infamous Safari Pose on top of Kordic. The coroner also asserted that the police all but ignored the medical signs of possible fatal pulmonary edema.

When the internal investigation by the Quebec Provincial Police ran into setbacks, a police cover-up was alleged by Paul Bouchard, lawyer for the Kordic family. The controversy intensified when an audio specialist later claimed that police tapes of the incident had been subsequently erased, cut up, or spliced. In February 1993, about five months into the public inquiry, the Kordic family filed a $1.6 million lawsuit against the police, the ambulance service, and the city of Quebec.

Suspicions of a conspiracy seemed confirmed just months later, when a Quebec government probe concluded that the police union's power was absolute, and often abusive and corrupt. In 1994 five Montreal policemen went on trial for assault causing bodily harm, charges arising from an incident in which taxi driver Richard Barnabe fell into a coma while in police custody.

In early 1995 Bouchard claimed that new evidence would further prove that police involvement in Kordic's death was criminally negligible. He asserted that the pending lawsuit would expose the doctoring of evidence as well as loopholes in police testimony. The Quebec Provincial Police offered to settle the suit out of court, and Bouchard accepted, knowing that it would help the embattled Kordic family put the entire affair behind them. Details about the new evidence were never revealed, however, because the settlement required that the lawyer not divulge any information. It was later speculated that the police had yelled obscenities at Kordic as he lay dying, and that offending officers later expressed guilt and regret over having caused his death.

THE NHL RESPONDS

The NHL narrowly avoided a public inquiry into drug use among its players when Quebec investigators decided not to subpoena league executives, or players and management with the Canadiens and Nordiques hockey clubs. Having deduced that at least some NHL players used cocaine and steroids, the public inquiry allowed that perhaps substance abuse existed on a larger scale than previously thought.

Legal obstacles, the inquiry acknowledged, prevented it from further investigating the matter. It was suggested that substance abuse in the NHL should be further probed, but league executives did not immediately take action. Five months after the inquiry's findings, however, the Quebec Major Junior Hockey League introduced a comprehensive policy to deal with alcohol- and drug-abuse.

The NHL did not seriously consider a comprehensive substance abuse policy until Gary Bettman succeeded Gil Stein as President in 1994. Bettman's argument that the NHL needed such a policy coincided with the problems encountered by Red Wings forward Bob Probert, who had a run-in with police and later tested positive for cocaine. The new league President was aware that Kordic, like many athletes, often ran into problems with alcohol and drugs only after turning pro, suggesting that part of the problem involved the coping pressures of big league sports.

A comprehensive substance abuse policy finally took shape by the mid-1990s, with attention focused on several distinct issues: education, access-confidentiality, after-care, alcohol-abuse treatment, three-strike approach, required treatment, prohibited substances, and program administration.

LEGACY: RISE AND FALL OF AN ENFORCER

There was no massive outpouring of grief in the world of pro hockey when 27-year-old bad boy John Kordic died. There were no official tributes to the fallen hockey player, nor did any of the NHL teams he played for establish awards, trophies or memorial funds in his name. It seemed that pro hockey wanted to quickly forget about John Kordic, perhaps fearing that the sport's darker side might be accurately reflected in Kordic's well-documented sub stance abuse battles, as well as the pressure he felt living up to his reputation as a fighter.

Kordic's death was largely the result of an aggravated physical state brought on by the ingestion of large amounts of cocaine and alcohol, combined with strong-armed police tactics. News coverage in Quebec has ensured that the tragedy will always be linked to allegations of brutality and misconduct on the part of police in Quebec, as well as neglect by ambulance and hospital personnel and a subsequent orchestrated cover-up.

Kordic's demise will also be invariably linked to alcohol- and drug-abuse. His substance abuse habits were largely rooted in his spiritual pain, which resulted from the inner conflict he felt over having to fight in order to make it in pro hockey. From his days as a junior star to his tenure in the NHL, Kordic was continually pressured by coaches and management to be a fighter, an enforcer.

Little attention seemed to be given to helping John develop his playing skills. This made the player very sad, particularly since he knew how much his father disapproved of the fighting. Kordic felt ashamed that he had let his dad down, and as an escape from his guilt and pain often turned to alcohol and drugs. He also turned to drugs such as steroids in order to maintain a massive physique, which he believed augmented his status as a fighter. He had graduated to steroids in order to keep his job in the NHL, an ultra-competitive league.

The great irony is that Kordic ingested steroids to keep his job as a hockey enforcer, but then abused alcohol and cocaine to escape the psychological pain of having to fulfill that role and ultimately let down his father. Ivan Kordic's death denied his son the chance to achieve any real closure on this inner conflict, and as a result John fell into a deeper cycle of substance abuse, one which eventually killed him.

John Kordic's tragic death compels one to consider what place, if any, fighting should have in pro hockey. How did a talented hockey player, who once tallied 78 points as a defenseman in the junior ranks, become a fighter with little hockey skills? It might be argued that there has long been a systemic problem in pro hockey, where coaches and management pressure certain young athletes to be fighters rather than hockey players. This problem seemed to reach its apex in the 1980s and early 1990s, when fighting in the game was glorified rather than discouraged.

The debate about the place of fighting in hockey rages on today – some people feel that it is a necessary outlet for the players in a rugged, physical game, and that it actually allows players to "blow off some steam" without resorting to more violent tactics. Others feel that fighting has no real place in the sport and that hockey's mass popularity has suffered as a result – these people feel that fighting should be banned from the sport. Perhaps a better understanding of the systemic problem of fighting in pro hockey will lead to a realistic solution.

Kordic's tragic death also makes one consider the problem of substance abuse in pro hockey. Athletes face enormous physical and psychological pressures in the extremely competitive world of pro sports, and as a form of escapism many of them seek solace in alcohol and drugs. Until recent years, these type of problems have not received the attention they merit. Like many other pro sports leagues, the NHL had no substance-abuse policy before the Kordic tragedy, but since then has been compelled to establish and further develop a comprehensive policy regarding the use of alcohol and drugs by its players. These problems are related to those involving sexual abuse. There continue to be widespread allegations that former Winterhawks owner Brian Shaw had sexual relations with Kordic, but these claims remain unsubstantiated.

Perhaps John's off-ice problems were initially related to his experiences in Portland. In recent years former NHLer Sheldon Kennedy has publicly admitted being sexually abused by Graham James, his former minor league coach. Kennedy's story received a lot of news coverage, and as a result there has been an increase in public pressure for more accountability. As a result, pro hockey policymakers have recently developed a more comprehensive sexual abuse policy.

AFTER KORDIC: RISE AND FALL OF OTHER ENFORCERS

In March 2002, almost a decade after Kordic's death, his good friend and former Nordiques teammate Bryan Fogarty also passed on, allegedly a result of physical ailments caused by alcohol and substance abuse. At the time of Kordic's own tragic end, the general consensus was that the tragedy resulted from his abuse of alcohol, cocaine, steroids, and/or other drugs, in tandem with injuries suffered during a prolonged physical altercation with Quebec City police. Also considered was the possibility that Kordic's dramatic demise was partly linked to concussions and other severe brain trauma he might have incurred, from blows to the head during those many fights.

Over the past two decades there has been a great increase in the frequency and severity of brain injuries suffered by players in contact sports such as hockey, football, and even soccer. This is invariably true at all levels of these sports, from bantam and midget all the way up to the big leagues. The risks, of course, are greater at the highest levels.

More than 20 former NFLers have posthumously been found to display CTE (Chronic Traumatic Encephalopathy), a degenerative brains disease caused by blunt trauma to the head. While alive, many of them experienced drug abuse issues, impulse control problems and impaired memory.[54] Degenerative brain disease has also been linked to the deaths of several former NHL players, including enforcers such as Reg Fleming and Bob Probert. The hockey world was hit particularly hard in 2011, when three current or former pugilists died: Derek Boogard (accidental overdose of alcohol and painkillers), Rick Rypien (depression-related) and Wade Belak (suicide).

Tragic incidents such as these soon prompted the NHL executive and well as individual teams to be more proactive in diagnosing and treating concussions and other brain injuries suffered by players. Former players also responded; in November of 2013 the first of five proposed class action lawsuits in regards to traumatic brain incidents was filed by over two dozen former NHLers against the league. It was just the start of a long ongoing legal battle on this issue between the NHL and its current and former players.

There is now widespread recognition that severe brain injuries in pro contact sports such as hockey need to be properly addressed and treated. It has all come much too late for John Kordic, of course, but hopefully increased progress will help avert other personal tragedies. In regards to the man himself, the spotlight on C.T.E. certainly sheds some light on the physical struggles and personal demons which the enforcer could not overcome, and makes him seem so much more human, and vulnerable, over twenty years later.

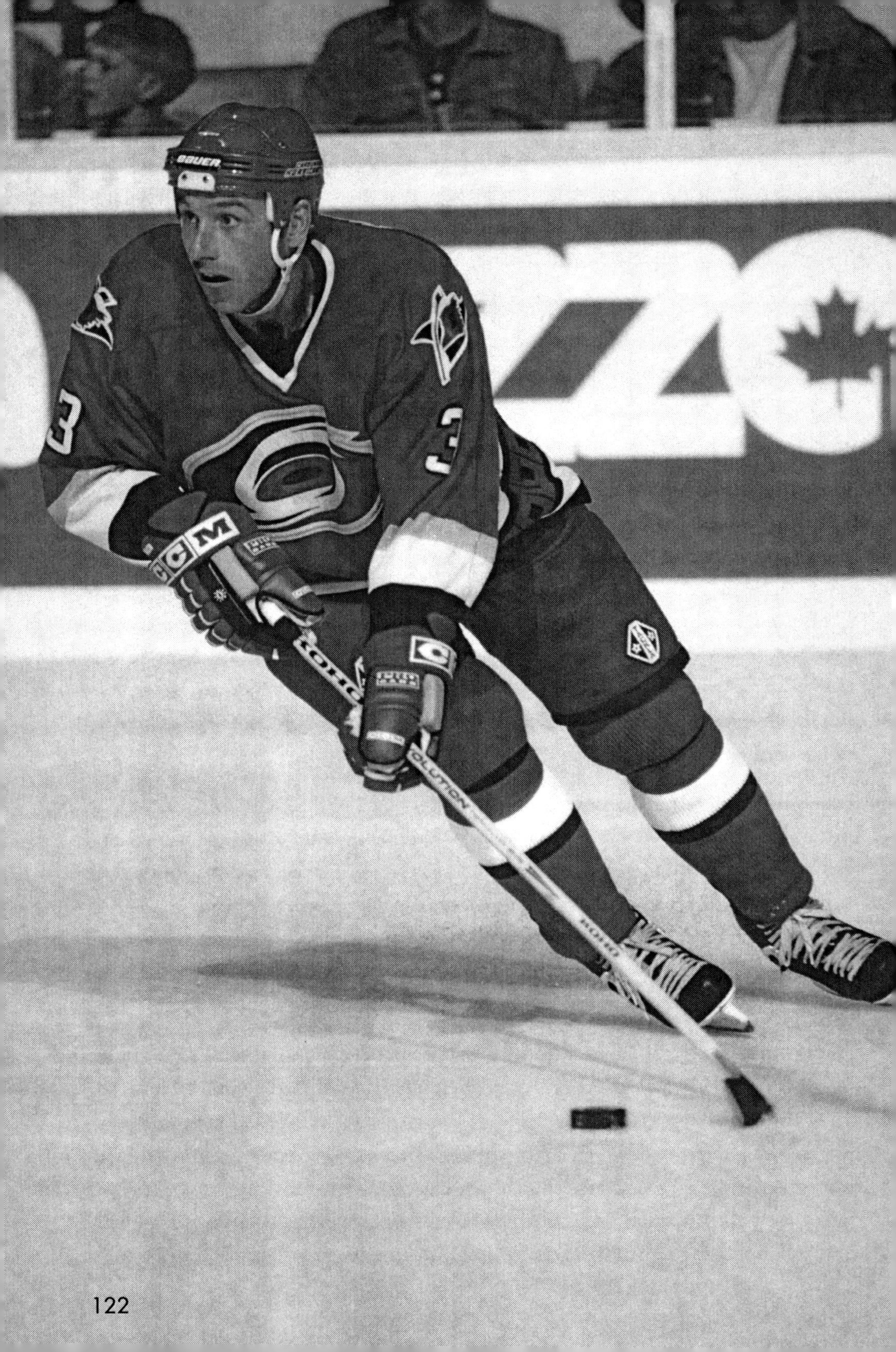
CCM

CHAPTER 6

1967 - 1999

STEVE CHIASSON

On May 8th, 1998, they gathered at the Cathedral of St.Pete's-in-chains in Peterborough, Ontario, to say good-bye to Steve Chiasson, journeyman NHL defenseman, loving husband and father. The standing-room only crowd attended a somber memorial service which celebrated the hockey player's life, just days after he had been instantly killed in a single-car accident outside Raleigh, North Carolina. Chiasson enjoyed a solid 13-year NHL career, playing with Detroit, Calgary, Hartford and then Carolina. Compiling 273 points in 503 games, the steady rearguard also played in the 1993 All-Star game, and represented Canada at the World Hockey Championships in 1987 and 1997. His sudden loss shocked and saddened the hockey world.

THE PRIDE OF PETERBOROUGH

Born April 14, 1967 in Barrie, Ontario, Steve grew up in Peterborough, where his family moved when he was a child. He started playing defense as a young boy and in 1982-83 joined the Pittsburgh Travellers of the Ontario Midget Hockey Association (OMHA). He scored 25 goals and had 60 points in just 40 games, but his rough play led to 120 penalty minutes. Chiasson advanced to the Guelph Platers of the Ontario Hockey League the next season, and by his second year was the league's top defenseman.

In 1985-86 he led the Platers to the OHL Championships and then to the Memorial Cup finals. Guelph won the Cup, and with five points in four games the defenseman was awarded The Stafford Smythe Memorial Trophy as the tournament's best player. Scouts for the Detroit Red Wings were impressed with

Steve's solid if unspectacular play, and by his developing offensive acumen. The Red Wings were in the midst of a massive rebuilding phase, emerging from the franchise's dark years - the 1970s and early 1980s. The club desperately needed good, capable rearguards to complement promising young forward like Steve Yzerman and Adam Oates. At 17 Chiasson was still an underage junior, but Detroit took a chance anyways and selected him as their third pick, 50th overall, in the 1995 NHL Entry Draft.

TICKET TO MOTOWN

Promoted to the Red Wings in 1986-87, Chiasson joined an NHL squad coming off one of the worst seasons in team history, desperate to change its sagging fortunes. Emerging young star Steve Yzerman had been injured for much of the previous campaign, and the team had earned the nickname "The Dead Things" with its horrible record of 17-57-6, last place overall in the NHL. Coach Harry Neale was fired halfway through the season, and former Wing defenseman Brad Park fared little better behind the bench. Determined to shake things up, new owner Mike Illitch hired former St. Louis Blues' coach Jacques Demers to motivate the befuddled players.

With young talent like Chiasson and Gerard Gallant added to the mix, the team emerged much stronger the next year. Yzerman played a full season, becoming one of the top scorers in the league, and the Wings posted a decent 34-36-10 record, good for second place in the Norris Division and a playoff spot. Detroit finished 38 points higher than it had in 1985-86, one of the largest improvements in NHL history. Pressed into regular action early on, Steve had acquitted himself well on the blueline, with his 45 points among rookie leaders. At 6 foot 1 and 205 pounds, he was the type of big, mobile defenseman the team needed. Chiasson was young, skated well, and played positional, hard-nosed hockey.

The resurgent Wings won their first two playoff series, advancing to the Western Conference finals against the mighty Edmonton Oilers. Chiasson was an anchor on defense in game one, capably handling the likes of stars Wayne Gretzky and Jarri Kurri as Detroit upset the Oilers in their rink. Their luck would not hold, however, as Edmonton won the next four games to take the series. The Wings' surprising playoff run had been the farthest a

Detroit squad had advanced in the post-season in over thirty years, and laid the groundwork for future success. As Detroit's most effective defenseman, Chiasson was an essential part of the plan.

Yzerman, later team captain, became good friends with Chiasson. 'We got along really well. We lived in Grosse Pointe (a suburb of Detroit) and drove back and forth to the rink and to the airport quite a bit," he recalled. "He was a great player to have on your team, he played hard and he fit in well with the team."[1] The steady if unspectacular defenseman was often under appreciated, but his teammates were aware of his no-nonsense approach. 'The one thing he used to say, and probably the best thing you could say, when things weren't going good and you'd have meetings to talk about it, he'd always say Shut up and play," Yzerman claimed. "He was a simple guy who never looked into things too much, didn't overanalyze things."[2]

With young players like Gerald Gallant and Bob Probert contributing, the Wings continued their strong play the next season, emerging as one of the league's stronger teams. With a 41-28-11 record and 93 points, Detroit easily captured the Norris Division, but the talented Chiasson was limited to just a couple of goals and 11 points in 29 games. In the post-season, the team won its first two series, advancing again to the Conference finals against the Oilers. Once more Edmonton defeated Detroit in five games.

In 1988-89 the Wings got off to a slow start but managed to stay ahead of the its weaker Norris opponents, Suffering a nagging groin injury, Steve also struggled early on, but gradually improved as the season wore on. He enjoyed his best game offensively on December first, when he had a goal and three assists in a win over the Quebec Nordiques. Soon after, Chiasson was sidelined by bruised ribs and, later, a sprained ankle. In sixty-five games, he still managed to lead all Red Wing defenseman with 12 goals and 47 points, and had 157 penalty minutes. Opponents took few liberties with the hard-nosed rearguard, whose tough defense often resulted in various ailments. Detroit had not enjoyed a stellar campaign, but it was still good enough for first in the Division. In the first playoff round, however, they lost to St, Louis.

Chiasson had a career-high 14 goals to go with 42 points the next year, but the team slipped significantly in the standings, finishing fifth and barely missing the playoffs. In 1990-91 the Wings rebounded slightly, spending much of the season battling for a post-season berth. Nagging injuries limited Chiasson's effectiveness, particularly offensively. In November, he re-injured his already sore knee, then soon after broke his ankle. "He was a guy who played hard and through some pretty serious injuries, some broken bones," Yzerman remembered. "He didn't complain too much about anything."[3]

The defenseman attempted to come back a month later, only to re-injure his ankle and subsequently miss 26 games. In 42 games, he managed to provide solid defense and still register 20 points, but management was concerned that the development of their oft-injured defenseman had stalled. Detroit exited early in the playoffs after finishing third in their division.

CHIASSON FINDS HIS GROVE

In 1991-92 Steve Chiasson and the Wings came of age. Re-injuring his right ankle early in the campaign, the defenseman returned after missing over a month and went on a seven-game point streak, with two goals and six assists. He finished with 10 goals and 32 points, helping Detroit post a 43-25-12 record and 98 points, the most recorded by a Red Wing team in forty years. Atop the Norris Division standings at the end of the season, Detroit won its opening playoff series before losing in the Division semi-finals.

The NHL increased the number of games from 80 to 84 the following year, perhaps Chiasson's finest. Having established himself as an emerging league power, the Wings got off to a quick start. Steve was briefly sidelined with a bruised thigh, but upon his return established himself defensively and as an offensive threat, recording a four-assist night against the Tampa Bay Lightning in December. He was getting a lot of power play time and, with Yzerman and young Russian star Sergei Fedorov down low, his passes were setting up goals.

Chiasson was selected to play in the 1993 All-Star Game in Montreal, a high scoring affair between the Wales and Campbell Conferences, won by the former, 16-6. It was a big thrill for Steve to be in the annual classic, at the time an honour not often bestowed on Wing defensemen. Playing virtually the whole year injury free, he had 12 goals, a career-high 62 points, and a solid plus-twenty-two rating. With 155 penalty minutes, he also continued to be known for his bruising play. The Wings traded for superstar defenseman Paul Coffey, acquiring the veteran all-star late in the season from the Los Angeles

Kings. Detroit enjoyed a late season surge and finished in second place, with 103 points, the most in franchise history. Goaltending was a weak spot in the post-season, however, and they lost a heart breaking Division semi-finals to Toronto.

Detroit continued its winning ways in 1993-94; firmly entrenched as an NHL powerhouse, pressure mounted in Motown for the Wings to finally bring home the Stanley Cup, last won in 1955. Rookie goalie Chris Osgood emerged as the club's top stopper, and with Yzerman, Fedorov and Keith Primeau no team was stronger down the middle. Chiasson and Coffey spearheaded the NHL's most potent power-play, and Detroit finished first in the newly-created Central Division.

For the first and only time Steve did not miss a regular season game, amassing 13 goals, 46 points and a career-high 238 shots on goal. In the playoffs Detroit faced the hard-working but much less talented San Jose Sharks, led by crafty veteran Russian star Igor Larionov. The Sharks forced a game seven at Joe Louis Arena in Detroit, then stunned the home crowd with a late goal on a play botched by Osgood, ending the Wings' season.

In the off-season Red Wings management was intent on trading for an established veteran netminder with playoff success. Although happy with the emergence of Osgood, the team felt that a more seasoned goalie was needed to have a realistic chance at winning the Stanley Cup. The solid play of Coffey on the blue line also lessened the need for Chiasson's services, particularly on the power play. On June 29th, Detroit traded him to the Calgary Flames for Mike Vernon, who had backstopped the Flames to the 1986 championship.

VETERAN ON THE FLAMES

The 1994-95 NHL regular season was postponed because of a labour strike, and the schedule was eventually cut from 84 to 48 games. Chiasson joined a strong Flames squad, loaded in offensive talent with Theoren Fleury, Joe Nieuwendyk and Gary Roberts, a close friend and teammate on the 1986 Memorial Cup-winning Guelph Platers. Providing his customary steady defense and helping to resurrect Calgary's power-play, Steve managed 25 points, and an impressive plus-ten rating. With only 39 penalty minutes, he had matured into a more emotionally controlled rearguard, still tough but with less of a penchant for needless infractions. The Flames finished first in the tough Pacific Division with 55 points, but were upset in the first playoff round.

Beset by minor ailments, Chiasson struggled both defensively and offensively early in his second year with Calgary, and injuries to other key players also hurt the team's performance. Recording his 300th career point against San Jose, less than two weeks later, on December 11th, the defenseman scored on a penalty shot against the Los Angeles Kings' Bryan Dafoe, the only one of his career.

With a four-game point streak late in the season, he finished second among Flames defenseman with eight goals and 33 points, 16 of those on the power-play. Ending up second in the division, Calgary lost their opening post-season round in four games, but Chiasson led the team in scoring with a couple of goals and an assist.

Injuries took a much heavier toll on both the rearguard and the team early in 1996-97; with a severely strained medial collateral ligament, Steve missed almost 20 games in the first half of the season, and Calgary struggled just to stay out of last place in their division. The Flames were well out of a playoff spot early, and the defenseman had managed just five goals and 16 points in 47 games, with an unimpressive minus-eleven rating. On March 5, Chiasson and a third-round draft pick were traded to the Hartford Whalers for defender Glen Featherston, forward Hnat Domenichelli, and two future draft picks.

NEW LIFE IN HARTFORD

The Whalers hoped that Chiasson could provide steady defense and occasionally contribute offensively. He scored a power-play marker in his very first contest, a win over the Montreal Canadiens, and was chosen the game's first star. Days later he recorded two assists against the Bruins; his surprisingly solid two-way play prompted the NHL to name him Player of the Month for March.

His confidence now fully restored, he recorded a goal and an assist against the Buffalo Sabres a few days later. Finishing the season with 14 points in his 18 games with the Whalers, Chiasson helped Hartford make a late surge for the playoffs, but the team finished fifth in the Northeast Division, out of the playoffs.

RELOCATION TO CAROLINA

Hartford Whalers owner Peter Karamanos had been trying to move the struggling franchise out of Connecticut since the early 1990s, having become frustrated with a combination of poor gate receipts, bad local television and marketing deals, and an unfavorable arena lease. He finally succeeded on June 25, 1997, when the NHL officially approved the move to North Carolina, where the team was renamed the Carolina Hurricanes.

Playing out of a geographically remote facility as it awaited final construction of a new state-of-the-art arena in downtown Raleigh, the 1997-98 Hurricanes struggled to sell tickets and to ice a strong team. Chiasson and former Wing teammate Coffey anchored the blue line and the power-play, and one of Steve's long-time friends, power forward Gary Roberts, joined the club prior to the start of the regular campaign. Having slowed down somewhat offensively, Steve still managed seven goals and 34 points. Carolina battled for a playoff spot, barely missing the post-season, but laying the groundwork on which to build its fan base.

THE FINAL SEASON

Chiasson and the Hurricanes got off to a strong start the next season, the club actually leading the Northeast Division early on. Injuries returned to haunt the veteran defenseman, when he was sidelined by a serious shoulder injury. He stubbornly came back too early, re-damaging his already battered shoulder three separate times in April and March, and was soon through for the regular season with a month still left on the schedule. In 28 games, he recorded nine points, the lowest total in his career, and a plus-six rating. In spite of the loss, Carolina made the playoffs and faced the Boston Bruins in the opening round.

With Chiasson's season apparently over, many observers were surprised when the rearguard announced himself ready to go on the eve of the post-season. Having come to rely on his veteran presence, the team was glad to have him back. "He was not the designated captain, but was understood as being the honorary captain," President and General Manager Jim Rutherford recalled. "He was the kind of guy everyone wanted to be around, certainly a big member with his teammates and a real ordinary guy that loved the game of hockey and loved the people around him."[4]

Not expected to put up much resistance against the stronger Bruins, the Hurricanes were resilient and the series was tied at two games apiece as it headed back to Carolina. Early in game five, Chiasson pinched in from the blueline and fired a slapshot past Bruins goalie Bryan Dafoe, giving the Canes a 1-0 lead. The game was tied 3-3 at the end of regulation, and it took Boston two overtime periods to finally end it. The Bruins then won 2-0 back on home ice, closing out the series.

The heartbreaking loss did not detract from what was a relatively successful season for the new franchise. Having battled back from injuries all season, Chiasson had established himself as one of the Hurricanes' most dependable defenseman, and with a goal and two assists tied Roberts in team playoff scoring.

After the loss in Boston, the team caught a late-night charter back to Raleigh. Spirits were high on the return leg, and team spokesman Chris Brown later recalled that two cases of beer, juice and assorted soft drinks were consumed by the players. Brown could not remember if Chiasson drank on the plane.[5] Roberts suggested to his teammates that they hold a team party back at his house, in a suburban area just north of Raleigh, but Rutherford was not aware of the plan.[6] 'We landed at one (in the morning)," he later claimed, "and it was my understanding that we were all heading home."[7] After the plane touched down, however, the players dispersed to their respective vehicles, and headed over to Roberts' house.

THE PARTY

The season over and the future of the franchise looking bright, most of the players were in an up-beat mood at the party. Like many of the Hurricanes, Chiasson was very tired, and very dehydrated, having logged more than forty minutes in the game five double-overtime loss, and another thirty minutes in game six. "He had lost ten pounds," teammate Kevin Dineen admitted, "and there was a lot of physical exhaustion there."[8] Around 3:30 a.m. Roberts wisely started arranging for taxi's to take several of the fading players home.

The host of the party was particularly concerned about Chiasson, and did not want him driving home. Informed that Steve was out in the garage with Dineen, smoking a cigar, Roberts found him and tried unsuccessfully to convince the uncooperative defenseman to wait for the taxis. "He made a bad judgement," Dineen asserted. "We were out in the garage, and he said, I'm ready to go home and see the kids. He was determined and stubborn enough to go home."[9] Dineen went upstairs to get someone to drive Chiasson home, but returned to find him already gone. "We saw the headlights of the car go out," Kevin said. "He was down there (the garage) by himself. He made a conscious decision to go home. His state was impaired."[10]

To this day, Roberts insists that everybody at the party did what they could to stop the rearguard from leaving:

> Every guy that was there wishes they could have done something more. If there was any indication at all that Steve Chiasson was ever thinking about driving home, we wouldn't have allowed it to happen. People wrote that we tried to stop him and he wouldn't listen, but that's not true. We would have tied him to the house before we would have let him drive home. One minute he was smoking a cigar in my garage, next thing you know he was in the car driving home.[11]

When it became obvious that Chiasson left in his truck, team captain Ron Francis promptly grabbed his cars keys, and departed to follow him. Francis, who had not been drinking any alcohol, lived on the same street and followed the same route the defenseman would have taken home. It was not a long drive, as Chiasson lived just minutes down the road from Roberts. Francis drove right past the accident site without even noticing it, only to discover that Steve's pick-up truck was not in the driveway. "Ronnie went home and called me and said Chase's car wasn't in the driveway, he must've parked it in the garage, but that's strange because he never parks in the garage," Roberts remembered. 'Then all of a sudden I heard the sirens. We were all waiting at my house and my wife called and said, Gary, you won't believe it. It's Chase's truck."[12]

THE ACCIDENT

Chiasson left the party in his 1996 Chevrolet pick-up truck just after 4 a.m., travelling down Falls of the Neuse Road. The weather was calm, but the dark and lonely two-lane road was not well-lit. Steve lost control of the vehicle while negotiating a curve, and when he tried to over-correct, the truck veered off the right side of the street, then to the left, before rolling over. Not wearing his seatbelt, Chiasson crashed through the front windshield and was killed instantly.

Arriving at the accident site shortly afterwards, the North Carolina State Highway Patrol could do little to save the defenseman, who was obviously dead. Trooper K.L. Horne, the first officer on the scene, noted the crash occurred around 4:15 a.m., but could not immediately confirm that alcohol was a contributing factor. Yet evidence at the crash site, according to Sergeant Jeff Winstead, indicated Chiasson had consumed too much alcohol.[13]

The festive atmosphere at Roberts' house had quickly become sad and somber, and those teammates who had hung around consoled each other in the wake of the shocking news. Many Hurricanes stayed past the break of dawn, awaiting more news and contacting their loved ones. The State Patrol also visited the house, and interviewed some of the players.

Hurricanes management hastily arranged an early morning news conference, and a clearly distraught Rutherford started off by saying that Chiasson's death "was a tragedy that is impossible to put into words."[14] Even more shaken was the coach, Paul Maurice, who at 32 was the same age as the late defenseman. "When you work together in our environment, you have a family among players and an extended family among wives and children that go to school together and play on sports teams together," he noted. "It's really an environment unlike any other...when a tragedy like this has happened, unfortunately...there's no other way to put it except for we've lost a member of our family. It's a very painful time for all of us."[15] Chiasson's defensive partner Glen Wesley added that the Hurricanes lost both a friend and teammate.[16]

NHL President Gary Bettman released a press statement around the same time. "This is a terrible tragedy. When a young life ends prematurely, when a young family loses a husband and father, words cannot begin to express our sorrow," he claimed. "Our thoughts and prayers are with Steve's wife Susan and their three children."[17] Detroit followed with its own. "Steve was a member of the Red Wings' family for several years and continued to be a close friend to individual players and staff, as well as the organization," the release stated. "We are deeply saddened by this tragic loss."[18]. The club was no stranger to such tragedy; in June 1997, team masseur Sergei Masakonov and Vladimir Konstantinov, Chiasson's former defensive partner, were both severely injured in a limo crash, returning home from a party celebrating the Wings' 1997 Stanley Cup win. Initially in critical condition, both men survived, but Konstantinov suffered head injuries and was confined to a wheelchair, his hockey career over.

The Highway Patrol released a preliminary report that afternoon, indicating that Steve was going 74 mph in a 55-mph zone and that alcohol was a probable factor in the accident. Results from his blood-alcohol test were pending. "That (alcohol) has not been ruled out," admitted State Trooper Horne, "but it has not been confirmed."[19] Spokeswoman Sara Kempin said that test results would not be available for two to three weeks, but indicated that alcohol was likely a determinant factor.[20]

THE DAY AFTER

An hour-long private memorial was held the next day at St. Andrew's Presbyterian Church, only minutes from the accident site. Several players were comforted by their wives or girlfriends as they entered the church, followed by team management, NHL President Bettman, and Director of hockey operations Colin Campbell. Among the last people in were Susan Chiasson and the three children, Mike, Ryan, and Stefanie. A large photograph of Steve in his Hurricanes uniform was situated on an easel, to the right of the altar. Approaching the front pew, two-year old Stefanie pointed at the photo and blurted, "There's my daddy"[21]. It was a poignant and painful moment.

Trying to remain composed, Susan addressed the congregation. As she spoke, Ray Sheppard, Steve's closest buddy, buried his head on his wife's shoulder. "I can just feel him here. He wasn't a hockey player, he was my best friend," she said. "He loved life. All of you go home and hug your significant other and kiss your children."[22]

Kevin Dineen talked of Chiasson the strong, silent leader. "Your dad spoke when he felt he had something to offer," Dineen noted, addressed the children. "He didn't speak just to be heard."[23] Finally, Sheppard, who roomed with Steve on the road, spoke of his honesty and integrity, but had trouble containing his emotions. "I'll take that with me for as long as I live," he claimed. "He'll be in our prayers forever. We should all be grateful for him."[24]

PETERBOROUGH MOURNS A NATIVE SON

Held May 8th at the Cathedral of St. Pete's-in-chains in Peterborough, Ontario, the funeral mass was attended by Steve's family and friends, his present and former teammates, Hurricanes management and others in the hockey world, including Bettman and Wayne Gretzky. Susan discussed how her pain had been eased somewhat by the love and support she received. 'Through God, Steve and all your prayers," she said as she fought back tears, "that pit in my stomach has been replaced by Steve's love and strength and his ability to always stay positive."[25]

Well aware he was the last person to see Chiasson alive, Dineen spoke about how the players all wished they'd done something differently. "This tragedy comes down to one person's bad judgement," he remarked. "It was a direct result of Steve's stubbornness and his desire to see his family."[26]

Susan Reinhart, the defenseman's older sister, recalled her big, little brother who outgrew his rock collection and their countless games of monopoly and scrabble. She also remembered how she often had to pull her younger sibling off an outdoor rink when he was just six years old. "He'd always say just five more minutes," she noted. "I also remember the chills we felt when he got to the NHL and his first game with the big boys."[27]

Having played with Chiasson at the 1993 all-star game, Gretzky admitted he long admired Steve's defense. "He was always tough for me to play against," Gretzky recalled. "He was a true competitor and played the game the way it should be played."[28]

After the mass, Chiasson's coffin was carried out by pallbearers Sheppard, Dineen, brother-in-law Tim Keating, and childhood friends Dean Haig, Jim Morton and Neil Wyath. The casket passed through a row of Minor Petes' players, which had formed an honour guard, a fitting tribute to the promising youngster who rose through the Petes' organization and became a solid NHL defenseman.

THE TOXICOLOGY REPORT

Results from Chiasson's blood-alcohol test returned sooner than expected. The state Medical Examiner's Office released toxicology findings on May 10th, concluding that excessive alcohol consumption was a major factor in the accident. Steve's blood-alcohol level was found to be 0.27, more than three times the legal limit of 0.08 in North Carolina. 'We always run a test for alcohol," supervisor Sharon Fuqua maintained. "If the police suspect drugs or they are found at the scene then we'll run more tests. That didn't happen."[29]

The state chapter of Mothers against Drunk Driving (M.A.D.D.) claimed that the 0.27 reading was one of the highest it had ever seen. "While we definitely feel for his family and friends, he was three and a half times over the legal limit," Executive Director Shannon Page noted. "This was not a first time drinker. We are grateful he didn't kill anyone else."[30] Page also added that there was a lesson to be learned from the tragedy. "We hope that his family and friends," she asked, "will take this opportunity, since he is so well known, to make other people aware that this is not an isolated incident and that everyone is affected by this."[31] One person certainly not surprised by the findings was Dineen, who had told Susan Chiasson to be prepared for the worst.

Upon finding out the results, the Hurricanes released a brief statement, "We are still in the healing process of losing a valued friend and teammate. "Obviously, we are disappointed in the toxicology report. However, a member of our hockey family lost his life and the feelings about this reach far beyond the hockey element of this tragedy."[32]

REMEMBERING CHIASSON

There was a sad, subdued atmosphere at the Hurricanes 1999-2000 training camp in Estero, North Carolina. The club decided to commemorate Chiasson by having a patch stitched onto game sweaters and a sticker placed onto the helmets, both bearing the defenseman's uniform number. "I walked in this morning and looked at my helmet and saw the No. 3 on there," said Paul Coffey. "It's an awful reminder. We just try to look at the good things. He unfortunately died at a young age, but he did a lot of great things sports-wise and has three beautiful children. That's the stuff we like to remember him by."[33]

In having the No. 3 patch stitched onto the jerseys, the organization had it placed on the left shoulder, next to the team logo. Roberts pointed out that the patch was as close to the heart as you can get it:

> I don't know how we can overcome it. I think we're closer because of it and that's not in a negative way or a positive way. The loss of Steve Chiasson is the toughest thing that this team individually has had to go through in our lives probably. I know throughout the summer there wasn't a day that went by that I never thought of Steve Chiasson... and hopefully this team will rise up to the challenge of having a real winning year and dedicating that year to Steve.[34]

Early in the season, Ron Francis talked about how the defenseman was a big part of the team, both on and off the ice. "A great competitor," he remembered. "It's very tough, You expect changes over the summer, guys leaving and playing in different cities, but this is totally different and very tough for us to deal with."[35]

Chiasson's life was celebrated in a pre-game ceremony on November 30th, before a home game against Calgary. Susan and the three children took part in a ceremonial face-off with Francis, Roberts and Wesley. Then addressing the supportive crowd, Susan related how exciting it was to return from Canada and be re-united with the extended NHL family. "I think because of everything that went down in May, it's nice to come back and have a little bit of closure and put things in perspective," she said. "Lots of people needed to know we're ok. We kind of left real quickly. We're doing ok."[36]

Susan also related that Steve was an amazing partner and father. "My children have such a great bond with him still. He was a good friend and great teammate and the most positive person I've met in my whole life," she claimed. "At death, life doesn't end, it just changes. I'm sort of learning to figure out what that means."[37]

Steve Chiasson's white home jersey hung in his empty dressing stall throughout 1999-2000, a solemn reminder of the fallen Hurricane. The team also established an award in his name, voted on by players; The Steve Chiasson Award is presented each year to the Hurricane "who best exemplifies determination and dedication, while proving to be an inspiration to teammates through his performance and his approach to the game." At the end of the regular season, defenseman Sean Hill became its first recipient.

ANGELS AMONG US

In December of 1999, Susan and the three children celebrated their first Christmas holiday season without Steve, but she claimed that he was really never too far away. "The kids are really close to him. Stephanie, in particular. Maybe because she's so little, but she sees things we don't see," his widow asserted. "Steve was an amazing daddy. My kids are lucky. It's awful, what happened, but they're ok. We move on. I just told them, Daddy lives in your heart, and he goes with you everywhere. We really believe that at death life doesn't end. It just changes. And let me tell you...there are angels among us."[38]

Susan felt that Steve's death was preventable on many levels. His surgically-repaired shoulder was so damaged that he should not have played that last game, she contended, but he wanted to prove he could still perform up to high standards, particularly since he had a new contract to negotiate in the summer. "He didn't want to sign with somebody just to bang the puck off the glass," she claimed. "He would have retired first. But that Sunday night, he knew. He knew everything was ok."[39]

Susan said that Chiasson was like the old-time players in his love of the game, but noted that he was very vulnerable that night. "There are incredible lessons to be learned from how and why Steve died," she added. "But there are also incredible lessons to be learned from how he lived."[40] After his death, Susan Chiasson helped keep his memory alive by raising over $200,000 for the construction of a memorial pond in Steve's name, to be located in a scenic park in his hometown of Peterborough.

LEGACY: THE DEPENDABLE DEFENSEMAN

Steve Chiasson is remembered by many in pro hockey as a steady if unspectacular defenseman who played a no-nonsense brand of hockey, a fierce competitor and team leader who would rather play than talk. Capable and reliable, he was a star defenseman in junior hockey, and became an anchor on the blueline in Detroit, Calgary, Hartford, and Carolina.

A loving husband and caring father to his three children, Chiasson always seemed to have a positive outlook on life. Although his life will be recalled within the context of his death from impaired driving, many will still remember the talented defenseman's impressive personal and professional achievements, in a productive but brief life.

Chiasson's legacy was revisited during the 2002 Stanley Cup Playoffs, when Carolina enjoyed unprecedented post-season success. Only nine Carolina players remained from the 1998-99 team, but the coach, Paul Maurice, believed that Steve's strong work ethic had left an indelible impression on them. "He was part of the core, and one year we had eight or nine guys playing with tough, tough injuries, but none would take themselves out," he recalled. "Steve was playing with a torn labrum in his shoulder, but he kept playing. That set a standard for the team that's still in the room."[41]

Maurice noted how Chiasson's tragic death compelled the team to grow and mature. "There have been a lot of sacrifices to get to this point in the history of the Hurricanes," he said, during the team's semi-finals series against the Toronto Maple Leafs.'We've been through a lot of adversity (in the 2002 playoffs), although it all pales in comparison to what happened to him (Steve). He was so willing to go through the pain of playing in Greensboro and everything else. That's my one regret. He wasn't able to experience all of this."[42]

Since Chiasson's death in 1999, the once-struggling franchise has turned things around, having moved away from its remote Greensboro location and into the ultra-modern Raleigh Entertainment and Sports Arena, located in the busy city's central core. The hockey team still faces heavy competition for sports fans in the state, where basketball and racing always remain popular, but its success in the 2002 Cup playoffs captured the hearts of its fans.

In 2006 the Carolina Hurricanes returned to the Stanley Cup finals, this time facing off against the Oilers. By then the Hurricanes roster had been completely made over and only one player remained from Steve's final season. Veteran defenseman Glen Wesley was the late rearguard's former defensive partner and one of his closest friends. When Carolina defeated Edmonton to capture the first Stanley Cup in team history it was a bittersweet moment for the grizzled Wesley, who was just a second-year player when Chiasson died.

After the Hurricanes finally reached their pinnacle in 2006, the team fell on hard times; as the 2014-15 season approached the team struggled to regain its bearings, having missed the playoffs seven of the past eight years, including the last five. Long-time President and General Manager Jim Rutherford had left the organization and ended up in Pittsburgh. The team continues its search for a dependable and steady veteran presence on defence, the kind of poise that Steve Chiasson so faithfully and dependably provided it some years ago.

END NOTES

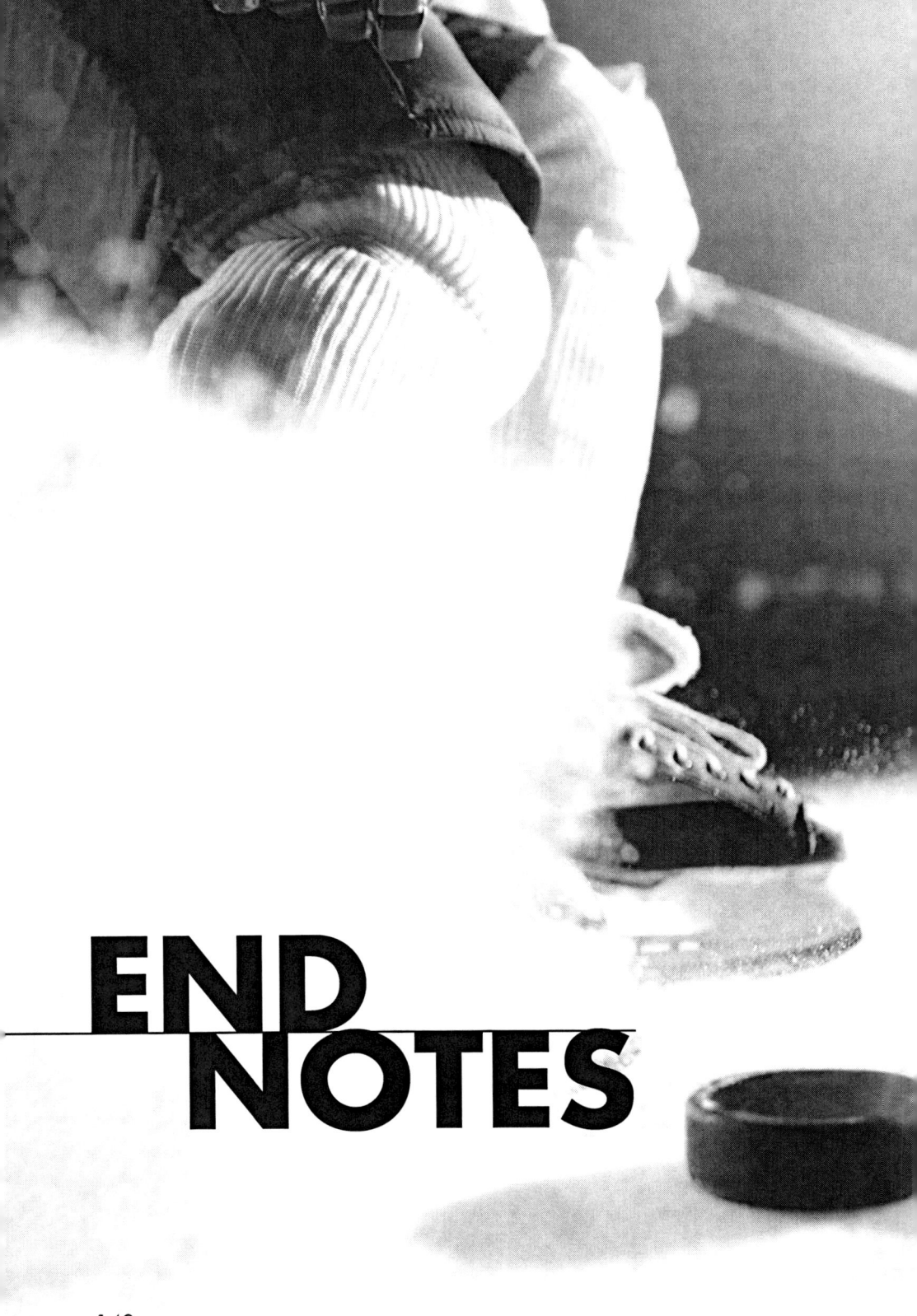

1. BILL MASTERTON

1. "Masterton dies of head injuries: First fatality in 51 years", St. Louis Dispatch. Tuesday, January 15, 1968
2. "Death ended Masterton's dream of big time hockey: Making Stars fulfilled lifelong ambition", St. Louis Dispatch, Tuesday, January 15, 1968
3. "Death ended Masterton's dream of big time hockey"
4. "Death ended Masterton's dream of big time hockey'
5. "Death ended Masterton's dream of big time hockey"
6. "Masterton dies of head injuries: First fatality in 51 years"
7. "Masterton dies of head injuries: First fatality in 51 years"
8. Gerald Eskenazi, Hockey, New York: Grosset & Dunlap Publishers, 1974, p. 103
9. "Masterton dies of head injuries: First fatality in 51 years"
10. "Masterton dies of head injuries: First fatality in 51 years"
11. "Masterton dies of head injuries: First fatality in 51 years"
12. Hockey, p. 104
13. "Masterton complained of headaches: Blair", The Globe & Mail, Wednesday, January 16, 1968, p. 29. Another source on role of Larry Cahan and Ron Harris is the Internet story, Joshua Atkins, Larry Cahan: A Biography, www.eprojectcompany.com, November 6, 2000
14. "Masterton complained of headaches: Blair", p. 29
15. "Masterton dies of head injuries: First fatality in 51 years"
16. Rex McLeod, "Fatal injury is hazard of pro hockey, NHL President says", The Globe & Mail, Wednesday, January 16, 1968, p. CI
17. "Masterton remains in critical condition", The Globe & Mail, Monday, January 14, 1968, p. 19. Also, please refer to Hockey, p. 104
18. "Masterton dies of head injuries: First fatality in 51 years"
19. "Masterton complained of headaches: Blair", p. 29
20. "Fatal injury is hazard of pro hockey, NHL President says", p. CI
21. Andrew Podnieks, The NHL All-Star Game: Fifty Years of the Great Tradition, Toronto: Harper Collins Publishers Ltd., 2000, p. 102
22. The NHL All-Star Game: Fifty Years of the Great Tradition, p. 102
23. "Fatal injury is hazard of pro hockey, NHL President says", p. CI
24. The NHL All-Star Game: Fifty Years of the Great Tradition, p. 103
25. Star Investigation: Bill Masterton, The Toronto Star, Saturday, May 28, 2011, A1
26. Star Investigation: Bill Masterton, The Toronto Star, Saturday, May 28, 2011, A1

27 Star Investigation: Bill Masterton, The Toronto Star, Saturday, May 28, 2011, A21

28 Star Investigation: Bill Masterton, The Toronto Star, Saturday, May 28, 2011, A1

29 Star Investigation: Bill Masterton, The Toronto Star, Saturday, May 28, 2011, A21

30 Star Investigation: Bill Masterton, The Toronto Star, Saturday, May 28, 2011, A1

31 Star Investigation: Bill Masterton, The Toronto Star, Saturday, May 28, 2011, A21

2. TERRY SAWCHUK

1 Dennis Dupuis, Sawchuk: The Troubles and Triumphs of the World's Greatest Goalie, Toronto: Stoddart Publishing, 1996, p. 4

2 Michael Benedict and D'Arcy Jenish, Canada On Ice: 50 Years of Great Hockey, Toronto: Penguin Books Canada, 1998, see Trent Frayne, "The Awful Ups and Downs of Terry Sawchuk", first published December 19, 1959, pages 178-185, p. 184 Also, see Internet story, George Johnson, "Sawchuk's life was great tragic," pages 1-3, ESPN.com, Wednesday, November 8, 2000, p. 1

3 Sawchuk: The Troubles and Triumphs of the World's Greatest Goalie, p. 8

4 Dick Beddoes, Dick Beddoes' Greatest Hockey Stories, Toronto: Macmillan of Canada, 1970, p. 118

5 Sawchuk: The Troubles and Triumphs of the World's Greatest Goalie, p. 30

6 Sawchuk: The Troubles and Triumphs of the World's Greatest Goalie, p. 33

7 Helene Eliot, "Triumph, Tragedy and Tenor filled Sawchuk's Life", The Sporting News, October 20, 2000. Also, see Sawchuk: The Troubles and Triumphs of the World's Greatest Goalie, p. 42

8 Sawchuk: The Troubles and Triumphs of the World's Greatest Goalie, p. 8

9 Brian Kendall, Shutout: The. Legend of Terry Sawchuk, Toronto: Penguin Books Canada, 1996, p. 61

10 Shutout: The Legend of Terry Sawchuk, p. 62

11 Sawchuk: The Troubles and Triumphs of the World's Greatest Goalie, p. 67

12 Sawchuk: The Troubles and Triumphs of the World's Greatest Goalie, p. 79

13 "Triumph, Tragedy and Terror filled Sawchuk's Life"; for the quote, refer to Sawchuk: The Troubles and Triumphs of the World's Greatest Goalie, p. 91. Details of the car accident may be found in Canada On Ice: 50 Years of Great Hockey, p. 184

14 Sawchuk: The Troubles and Triumphs of the World's Greatest Goalie, p. 94

15 Sawchuk: The Troubles and Triumphs of the World's Greatest Goalie, p. 105

16 Sawchuk: The Troubles and Triumphs of the World's Greatest Goalie, p. 106
17 Canada On Ice: 50 Years of Great Hockey, p. 179
18 Canada On Ice: 50 Years of Great Hockey, p. 181
19 Canada On Ice: 50 Years of Great Hockey, p. 180
20 "Sawchuk's life was great, tragic", p. 1
21 Sawchuk: The Troubles and Triumphs of the World's Greatest Goalie, p. 145
22 Sawchuk: The Troubles and Triumphs of the World's Greatest Goalie, p. 148
23 Shutout: The Legend of Terry Sawchuk. p. 159
24 Sawchuk: The Troubles and Triumphs of the World's Greatest Goalie, p. 155
25 Sawchuk: The Troubles and Triumphs of the World's Greatest Goalie, p. 155
26 Sawchuk: The Troubles and Triumphs of the World's Greatest Goalie, p. 160
27 Shutout: The Legend of Terry Sawchuk. p. 179
28 Shutout: The Legend of Terry Sawchuk. p. 184
29 Shutout: The Legend of Terry Sawchuk. p. 190
30 Shutout: The Legend of Terry Sawchuk. p. 190
31 Stephen Cole, The Last Hurrah: A Celebration of Hockey's Great Season: 66-67, Toronto: Penguin Books Canada, 1995
32 Dick Beddoes' Greatest Hockey Stories, see Terry Sawchuk, p. 117-122, p. 121
33 Kevin Allen and Bob Duff, Without Fear: Hockey's 50 Greatest Goaltenders, Chicago, Illinois: Triumph Books, 2002, "Terry Sawchuk", p. 177-185, p. 181 Also, see also Dick Beddoes' Greatest Hockey Stories, p. 121
34 Without Fear: Hockey's 50 Greatest Goaltenders, p. 181
35 See both the Sawchuk and Shutout bios, pages 215 & 217 respectively
36 Sawchuk: The Troubles and Triumphs of the World's Greatest Goalie, p. 215
37 Sawchuk: The Troubles and Triumphs of the World's Greatest Goalie, p. 220
38 Sawchuk: The Troubles and Triumphs of the World's Greatest Goalie, p. 220
39 Shutout: The Legend of Terry Sawchuk. p. 224
40 Sawchuk: The Troubles and Triumphs of the World's Greatest Goalie, p. 231
41 Sawchuk: The Troubles and Triumphs of the World's Greatest Goalie, p. 232
42 Shutout: The Legend of Terry Sawchuk. p. 227
43 Sawchuk: The Troubles and Triumphs of the World's Greatest Goalie, p. 242
44 Sawchuk: The Troubles and Triumphs of the. World's Greatest Goalie, p. 240
45 Shutout: The Legend of Terry Sawchuk. p. 229
46 Sawchuk: The Troubles and Triumphs of the World's Greatest Goalie, p. 249
47 Shutout: The Legend of Terry Sawchuk. p. 230
48 Sawchuk: The Troubles and Triumphs of the World's Greatest Goalie, p. 257

49 Shutout: The Legend of Terry Sawchuk. p. 234

50 Sawchuk: The Troubles and Triumphs of the World's Greatest Goalie, p. 258

51 Shutout: The Legend of Terry Sawchuk. p. 235-236

52 Shutout: The Legend of Terry Sawchuk. p. 237

53 Sawchuk: The Troubles and Triumphs of the World's Greatest Goalie, p. 262

54 Shutout: The Legend of Terry Sawchuk. p. 239

55 Sawchuk: The Troubles and Triumphs of the World's Greatest Goalie, p. 262

56 Shutout: The Legend of Terry Sawchuk. p. 258

57 Shutout: The Legend of Terry Sawchuk. p. 239

58 Shutout: The Legend. of Terry Sawchuk. p. 239

59 Sawchuk: The Troubles and Triumphs of the World's Greatest Goalie, p. 267. Please note that some details of his death were reported in "Terry Sawchuk, regarded as one of the best in game over 21 seasons in the NHL", The Globe & Mail, Monday, June 1, 1970, p. 17

60 Shutout: The Legend of Terry Sawchuk. p. 240

61 Shutout: The Legend of Terry Sawchuk. p. 240

62 Shutout: The Legend of Terry Sawchuk. p. 240

63 Sawchuk: The Troubles and Triumphs of the World's Greatest Goalie, p. 270

64 Sawchuk: The Troubles and Triumphs of the World's Greatest Goalie, p. 270

65 Sawchuk: The Troubles and Triumphs of the World's Greatest Goalie, p. 271

66 Sawchuk: The Troubles and Triumphs of the World's Greatest Goalie, p. 272

67 Sawchuk: The Troubles and Triumphs of the World's Greatest Goalie, p. 272

68 Sawchuk: The Troubles and Triumphs of the World's Greatest Goalie, p. 272

69 Shutout: The Legend of Terry Sawchuk. p. 244

70 Shutout: The Legend of Terry Sawchuk. p. 242

71 Sawchuk: The Troubles and Triumphs of the World's Greatest Goalie, p. 275

72 Sawchuk: The Troubles and Triumphs of the World's Greatest Goalie, p. 275

73 Sawchuk: The Troubles and Triumphs of the World's Greatest Goalie, p. 278

74 Dick Chubry, "St. Patrick a student of Sawchuk: Roy reading up on Legendary Goalie", pages 1-4, Edmonton Sun, Friday, January 14, 2000, p. 1

75 Karen Price, "Sawchuk's son in group honoring Roy for record," The Daily Camera, Denver, Colorado, October 21, 2000, p. 1

76 "St. Patrick a student of Sawchuk: Roy reading up on Legendary Goalie", p. 2

77 "Sawchuk's life was great, tragic", p. 2

78 "Sawchuk's life was great, traic,", p. 3

79 Without Fear: Hockey's 50 Greatest Goaltenders, p. 182

80 Without Fear: Hockey's 50 Greatest Goaltenders, p. 182

81 Without Fear: Hockey's 50 Greatest Goaltenders, p. 180
82 Without Fear: Hockey's 50 Greatest Goaltenders, p. 180
83 Interview between author and Lorne Worsley, Travelodge Hotel, Toronto, Ontario, Canada, Sunday, April 13, 2002
84 "Sawchuk's life was tragic, great", p. 2
85 Jo-Ann Barnes, "Jerry Sawchuk works to be dad he never had in Terry", pages. 1-9
86 The Detroit Free Press, June 17, 1999, pages 5-6
87 Interview with Ben Woit, north Toronto, Ontario, Canada, January 2014
88 Interview with Ben Woit, north Toronto, Ontario, Canada, January 2014

3. TIM HORTON

1 Television Documentary, "Life and Times: Tim Horton", CBC-TV, Broadcast on February 13, 2001
2 Douglas Hunter, Open Ice: The Tim Horton Story, Toronto: Penguin Books Canada Ltd., 1994, p. 13
3 Open Ice: The Tim Horton Story, p. 54
4 William Houston, Inside Maple Leaf Gardens, Scarborough, Ont.: McGraw-Hill Ryerson Ltd., 1989
5 Open Ice: The Tim Horton Story, p. 104
6 "Life and Times: Tim Horton"
7 Open Ice: The Tim Horton Story, pages 154-155
8 Internet information page, Tim Horton, Buffalo Sabres Alumni Association, 1999
9 Open Ice: The Tim Horton Story, p. 185
10 "From Cochrane to Carlton Street: Horton's rise to the top", Craig McInnis, Editor, Remembering Tim Horton: A Celebration, Toronto: Stoddart Publishing, 2000, p. 23
11 "Life and Times: Tim Horton"
12 Open ice: The Tim Horton Story, p. 197
13 Frank Orr, "Remembering the Tim Horton Bear Hug: I heard from ribs groan...", from Remembering Tim Horton: A Celebration, p. 38
14 Inside Maple Leaf Gardens, p. 105
15 "From Cochrane to Carlton Street: Horton's rise to the top", Craig McInnis, Editor, Remembering Tim Horton: A Celebration
16 "Life and Times: Tim Horton"

145

17 Punch Imlach and Scott Young, Punch Imlach's own story: Hockey is a battle, Toronto: Macmillan and Co., 1969, p. 122
18 Inside Maple Leaf Gardens, p. 55
19 Punch Imlach's own story: Hockey is a battle, pages 140-141
20 Inside Maple Leaf Gardens, p. 57
21 Stephen Cole, The Last Hurrah: A Celebration of Hockey's Greatest Season: '66-'67, Toronto: Penguin Books Canada Ltd., 1995, pages 334-335
22 Open Ice: The Tim Horton Story, p. 324
23 "Life and Times: Tim Horton"
24 "Life and Times: Tim Horton"
25 Mitch Potter, "Memories of a young fan: Growing up with Tim," from Remembering Tim Horton: A Celebration, p. 64
26 Open Ice: The Tim Horton Story, p. 329
27 Open Ice: The Tim Horton Story, p. 331
28 Open Ice: The Tim Horton Story, p. 343
29 Open Ice: The Tim Horton Story, p. 348
30 Open Ice: The Tim Horton Story, p. 369
31 Doug Herod, "Tim becomes a Sabre: Stealing a play from Toronto's Playbook," from Remembering Tim Horton: A Celebration, p. 107
32 Open Ice: The Tim Horton Story, p. 385
33 "Life and Times: Tim Horton". Also, see Open Ice: The Tim Horton Story, p. 390
34 "Life and Times: Tim Horton"
35 Dick Beddoes, "Buffalo Sabres' defenseman killed in car crash," The Globe & Mail, Friday, February 22, 1974, p. 29
36 "Buffalo Sabres' defenseman killed in car crash," p. 29
37 Open Ice: The Tim Horton Story, p. 404
38 Open Ice: The Tim Horton Story, p. 405
39 Open Ice: The Tim Horton Story, p. 413
40 Open Ice: The Tim Horton Story, p. 413-44
41 Open Ice: The Tim Horton Story, p. 414
42 Open Ice: The Tim Horton Story, p. 415. Author Douglas Hunter tried to obtain accident report from Ontario's Ministry of Transportation but reports are routinely kept on record for only ten years before being destroyed or thrown out.
43 Hunter discusses details in his book's last chapter, on page 415.
44 Open Ice: The Tim Horton Story, p. 417

45	Open Ice: The Tim Horton Story, p. 417
46	"Remembering the Tim Horton Bear Hug," from Remembering Tim Horton: A Celebration, p. 38
47	"Life and Times: Tim Horton"
48	"Buffalo Sabres' defenseman killed in car crash," p. 29
49	"Buffalo Sabres' defenseman killed in car crash," p. 29
50	"Buffalo Sabres' defenseman killed in car crash," p. 29
51	"Buffalo Sabres' defenseman killed in car crash," p. 29
52	Open Ice: The Tim Horton Story, p. 417
53	Open Ice: The Tim Horton Story, p. 417
54	"Highlights of Tim Horton," from Remembering Tim Horton: A Celebration.
55	Open Ice: The Tim Horton Story, p. 406

4. PELLE LINDBERGH

1	Internet story, Bill Meltzer, "Pelle Lindbergh", www.NHLhockeyjerseys.com
2	Lew Brown,"Lindbergh tragedy with him every day", Philadelphia Daily News, Nov. 20, 2000
3	"Lindbergh tragedy with him every day"
4	"Lindbergh tragedy with him every day"
5	Associated Press, "Doctors giving up on injured Flyer", The Globe & Mail, Monday, Nov. 11, 1985, p. CI
6	"Doctors giving up on injured Flyer", p. CI
7	"Lindbergh was heart of Flyers", The Toronto Star, Monday, November 11, 1985, p. Bi
8	"Doctors giving up on injured Flyer", p. Cl
9	"Doctors giving up on injured Flyer", p. Cl
10	"Pelle Lindbergh"
11	"Lindbergh was heart of Flyers", p. B1
12	"Lindbergh was heart of Flyers", p. B1
13	Internet tribute page, "Tribute to Lindbergh", www.members.tripod.com; internet story by by Wayne Fish, "Fallen friend remembered", at www.phillyBurbs.com, October 6, 2000
14	E.W. Swift, "Coping with a death in the family", Sports Illustrated, Dec. 2, 1985, Vol. 63, No. 25, pages 30-38, see pages 30 and 38 for two distinct quotes.
15	"Doctors giving up on injured Flyer", p. Cl
16	"Doctors giving up on injured Flyer", p. Cl
17	"Lindbergh tragedy with him every day"

18   "Pelle Lindbergh"
19   "Coping with a death in the family", p. 38
20   "Coping with a death in the family", p. 32-33
21   "Coping with a death in the family", p. 38
22   "Lindbergh tragedy with him every day"
23   "Lindbergh tragedy with him every day"
24   "Lindbergh tragedy with him every day"
25   "Lindbergh tragedy with him every day"
26   "Lindbergh tragedy with him every day"
27   "Lindbergh tragedy with him every day"
28   "Lindbergh tragedy with him every day"
29   "Lindbergh tragedy with him every day"
30   "Fallen friend remembered"
31   "Fallen friend remembered"
32   "Lindbergh tragedy with him every day"
33   "Lindbergh tragedy with him every day"
34   "Lindbergh tragedy with him every day"
35   "Doctors giving up on injured Flyer", p. Cl

5. JOHN KORDIC

1   Mark Zwolinski, The John Kordic Story, Toronto: Macmillan Canada, 1995, p. 4
2   The John Kordic Story, pages 17-32
3   The John Kordic Story, pages 17-32
4   Internet story, Joi Fwd, "The darker side of Hockey: A Tribute to John Kordic", pages 1-5, www.allsports.com, March 22, 1997, p. 1
5   The John Kordic Story, p. 55
6   Internet story, J. Gill, "Tragedy of a Hockey Player: John Kordic", pages 1-6, www. Njcc.com, March 6, 2001, p. 2
7   The John Kordic Story, p. 5'7
8   The John Kordic Story, p. 58
9   The John Kordic Story, p. 64
10 "Tragedy of a Hockey Player: John Kordic", p. 2
11 Jon Scher, "Death of a Goon", Sports Illustrated, April 24, 1992, Vol. 77, No. 8, p. 32-39, p. 33. Also, see "Tragedy of a Hockey Player: John Kordic", p2

12 Jon Scher, "Death of a Goon", Sports Illustrated, April 24, 1992, Vol. 77, No. 8, p. 32-39, p. 33. Also, see "Tragedy of a Hockey Player: John Kordic", p2
13 Jon Scher, "Death of a Goon", Sports Illustrated, April 24, 1992, Vol. 77, No. 8, p. 32-39, p. 33. Also, see "Tragedy of a Hockey Player: John Kordic", p2
14 The John Kordic Story, p. 64
15 "Tragedy of a Hockey Player: John Kordic", p.3
16 The John Kordic Story, p. 99
17 Internet story, "The wild misfits in hockey history", pages 1-3, www.interlog.com, March 6, 2001, p. 1
18 The John Kordic Story, p. 109
19 "The wild misfits in hockey history", p. 3
20 "The wild misfits in hockey history", p. 3
21 "Tragedy of a Hockey Player: John Kordic", p.3
22 The John Kordic Story, pages 124-125
23 The John Kordic Story, p. 129
24 The John Kordic Story, p. 131
25 The John Kordic Story, p. 138
26 The John Kordic Story, p. 130
27 The John Kordic Story, p. 143
28 "Tragedy of a Hockey Player: John Kordic", p.4
29 The John Kordic Story, p. 129
30 "Tragedy of a Hockey Player: John Kordic", p.4
31 Home Videotape Program, "Tough Guys' Hockey Fights", Copyright NHL. There is actually a section on the tape where John Kordic is interviewed.
32 The John Kordic Story, p. 161
33 "The wild misfits in hockey history", p. 3
34 "The wild misfits in hockey history", p. 3
35 "Death of a Goon", p. 32
36 David Shoalts, Canadian Press Reporter, "Kordic's death a microcosm of his career", The Globe & Mail, Monday, August 10, 1992, p. Cl
37 "Kordic's death a microcosm of his career"
38 "Death of a Goon", p. 36
39 "Death of a Goon", p. 38
40 "Death of a Goon", p. 38
41 "Death of a Goon", p. 36
42 "Kordic's death a microcosm of his career"

43 "Death of a Goon", p. 36
44 Damien Cox, "Kordic remembered as troubled, tormented", The Toronto Star, Monday, August 10, 1992, p. D1
45 "Death of a Goon", p. 33
46 "Death of a Goon", p. 33
47 "Death of a Goon", p. 36
48 "Kordic remembered as troubled, tormented"
49 "Death of a Goon"
50 "Death of a Goon"
51 The John Kordic Story, p. 184
52 The John Kordic Story, chapter 31, pages 193-204. This chapter contains details on the public inquiry findings into John Kordic's death. The inquiry was launched by the Quebec Provincial Government.
53 The John Kordic Story, p. 194
54 John Branch, Hockey Players' Death Pose a Tragic Riddle, New York Times, September 1, 2011

6. STEVE CHIASSON

1 Internet article, Steve Yzerman, "Daily Diary", The Sporting News, pages 1-2, www.sportingnews.com, May 10, 1999, p. 1
2 Steve Yzerman, "Daily Diary", p. 2
3 Steve Yzerman, "Daily Diary", p. 2
4 Internet story, "Hurricanes D Steve Chiasson killed in truck accident", Associated Press, pages 1-2, www.sportsyahoo.com, Monday, May 3, 1999, p. 1
5 Internet story, "Not belted in: Intoxication, speeding cited as factors in Chiasson crash", Associated Press, pages 1-3, www.sportsillustrated.com, Tuesday, May 4, 1999, p. 1
6 Ken Campbell, "Roberts coping with tragedy", The Toronto Star, April 15, 2001, E2
7 "Hurricanes D Steve Chiasson killed in truck accident", p. 2
8 Internet story; 'Tests show Chiasson was driving drunk", Associated Press, pages 1-3, www.sportsillustrated.cnn.com, May 10, 1999 p. 1
9 'Tests show Chiasson was driving drunk', p. 1
10 'Tests show Chiasson was driving drunk", p. 2
11 "Roberts coping with tragedy"
12 "Roberts coping with tragedy"
13 Internet story, Tom Foreman Jr., "Carolina's Chiasson killed in auto accident", Associated Press, pages 1-2, www.washingtonpost.com, May 3, 1999, p. 1

14 Internet story, "Chiasson killed in traffic accident", Associated Press, pages 1-3, www.sportsillustrated.cnn.com, May 4, 1999, p. 1
15 "Not belted in: Intoxication, speeding cited as factors in Chiasson crash"
16 "Hurricanes D Steve Chiasson killed in truck accident"
17 "Chiasson killed in traffic accident"
18 Internet story, "Hurricanes D Steve Chiasson killed", Associated Press, pages 1-2, www.sportsillustrated.cnn.com, May 3, 1999, p. 2
19 "Hurricanes D Steve Chiasson killed in truck accident"
20 "Chiasson killed in traffic accident"
21 Internet story, "Steve Chiasson's zest for life remembered", Associated Press, pages 1-4, vwvw.sportsillustrated.cnn.com, May 5, 1999, p. 2
22 "Steve Chiasson's zest for life remembered"
23 "Steve Chiasson's zest for life remembered"
24 "Steve Chiasson's zest for life remembered"
25 Internet story, "Chiasson celebrated at funeral", Associated Press, pages 1-3, www.sportingnews.com, May 8, 1999, p. 1
26 "Chiasson celebrated at funeral"
27 "Chiasson celebrated at funeral"
28 "Chiasson celebrated at funeral"
29 "Tests show Chiasson was driving drunk", p. 2
30 "Tests show Chiasson was driving drunk", p. 3
31 Internet story, "Tests show Chiasson was drunk", Associated Press, pages 1-3, www.sportingnews.com, May 10, 1999 p. 1
32 "Tests show Chiasson was driving drunk", p. 3
33 Internet story, Greg Hardwig, "Hurricanes remember Chiasson", Naples Daily News, September 8, 1999
34 "Hurricanes remember Chiasson"
35 "Hurricanes remember Chiasson"
36 Internet story, "Chiasson remembered in pre-game ceremony", Associated Press, pages 1-2, The Sporting News, www.sportingnews.com, Nov. 1999, p. 2
37 "Chiasson remembered in pre-game ceremony"
38 Internet story, Keith Gave, "Fatherless Chiasson children getting through the holidays", pages 1-3, www.sportsline.com, December 23, 1999, p. 1
39 "Fatherless Chiasson children getting through the holidays"
40 "Fatherless Chiasson children getting through the holidays"
41 Damien Cox, "Memories of Chiasson thrive in Carolina", p. E2, The Toronto Star, Saturday, May 1 8, 2002
42 "Memories of Chiasson thrive in Carolina"

PLAYER STATISTICS

BILL MASTERTON

Position: Center
Shoots: Right
Height: 5'10"
Weight: 170 lbs

Born: August 13, 1938
      Winnipeg, Manitoba, Canada
Died: January 15, 1968
      St. Paul-Minneapolis, Minnesota, USA

REGULAR SEASON

Year	Team	League	GP	G	A	PTS	PIM
55-56	St. Boniface	MJHL	22	23	26	49	16
	St. Boniface	Mem. Cup	6	3	5	8	2
56-57	St. Boniface	MJHL	30	23	30	53	16
57-58	U. of Denver	WCHA	Freshman - Did not play			
58-59	U. of Denver	WCHA	23	21	28	49	6
59-60	U. of Denver	WCHA	34	21	46	67	2
60-61	U. of Denver	WCHA	34	24	36	60	4
61-62	Hull-Ottawa	EPHL	65	31	35	66	18
62-63	Cleveland	AHL	72	27	56	82	12
63-64	Reinstated as Amateur						
64-65	Rochester	USHL	Statistics are not available			
65-66	St. Paul	USHL	30	27	40	67	6
66-67	U.S.A.	National Team	21	10	29	39	4
67-68	Minnesota	NHL	38	4	8	12	4
ONE (1) NHL SEASON			**38**	**4**	**8**	**12**	**4**

WCHA First All-Star Team, 59-60, 60-61

NCAA West First All- American Team, 59-60, 60-61 NCAA Championship All-Tournament Team, 60-61 NCAA Championship Tournament MVP, 60-61

The Bill Masterton Memorial Trophy is awarded annually to the NHL Player best Exemplifying perseverance, dedication and sportsmanship in hockey.

TERRENCE GORDON SAWCHUK

Position: Goaltender
Catches: Left
Height: 5'11"
Weight: 195 lbs

Born: December 28, 1929
Winnipeg, Manitoba, Canada,

Died: May 31, 1970
New York City, New York, U.S.A.

REGULAR SEASON

Year	Team	League	GP	W	L	T	GA	GAA	SO
45-46	Winnipeg	MJHL	10				58	5.80	
46-47	Galt	OHA	30				94	3.13	
47-48	Windsor	OHA	4				11	2.75	
	Spitfires	IHL	3	3	0	0	5	1.67	
	Omaha	USHL	54	30	18	5	174	3.21	
48-49	Indianapolis	AHL	67				205	3.06	
49-50	Indianapolis	AHL	51	31	20	10	188	3.08	
	Detroit	NHL	7	4	3	0	16	2.29	1
50-51	Detroit	NHL	70	44	13	13	139	1.99	11
51-52	Detroit	NHL	70	44	14	12	133	1.90	12
52-53	Detroit	NHL	63	32	15	16	120	1.90	9
53-54	Detroit	NHL	67	35	19	13	129	1.93	12
54-55	Detroit	NHL	68	40	17	11	132	1.94	12
55-56	Boston	NHL	68	22	33	13	181	2.66	9
56-57	Boston	NHL	34	18	10	6	81	2.38	2
57-58	Detroit	NHL	70	29	29	12	207	2.96	3
58-59	Detroit	NHL	67	23	36	8	209	3.12	5
59-60	Detroit	NHL	58	24	20	14	156	2.69	5
60-61	Detroit	NHL	37	12	16	8	113	3,17	2
61-62	Detroit	NHL	43	14	21	8	143	3.33	5
62-63	Detroit	NHL	48	22	16	7	119	2.48	3
63-64	Detroit	NHL	53	25	20	7	138	2.60	5
64-65	Toronto	NHL	36	17	13	6	92	2.56	1
65-66	Toronto	NHL	27	10	11	3	80	3.16	1
66-67	Toronto	NHL	28	15	5	4	66	2.81	2
67-68	Los Angeles	NHL	36	11	14	6	99	3.07	2
68-69	Detroit	NHL	13	3	4	3	28	2.62	0
69-70	New York	NHL	8	3	1	2	20	2.91	1
TWENTY-ONE (21) NHL SEASONS			971	447	330	172	2401	2.52	103

POST-SEASON

Year	Team	League	GP	W	L	GA	GAA	SO
45-46	Winnipeg	MJHL	2	0	2	12	6.00	
46-47	Galt	OHA	2	0	2	9	4.32	
47-48	Omaha	USHL	3	1	2	9	3.00	
48-49	Indianapolis	AHL	2	0	2	9	4.50	
49-50	Indianapolis	AHL	8	8	0	12	1.50	
50-51	Detroit	NHL	6	2	4	13	1.68	1
51-52	Detroit	NHL	8	8	0	5	0.63	4
52-53	Detroit	NHL	6	2	4	21	3.39	1
53-54	Detroit	NHL	12	8	4	20	1.60	2
54-55	Detroit	NHL	11	8	3	26	2.36	1
55-56	Boston	NHL						
56-57	Boston	NHL						
57-58	Detroit	NHL	4	0	4	19	4.52	0
58-59	Detroit	NHL						
59-60	Detroit	NHL	6	2	4	20	2.96	0
60-61	Detroit	NHL	8	5	3	18	2.32	1
61-62	Detroit	NHL						
62-63	Detroit	NHL	11	5	6	36	3.27	0
63-64	Detroit	NHL	13	6	5	31	2.75	1
64-65	Toronto	NHL	1	0	1	3	3.00	0
65-66	Toronto	NHL	2	0	2	6	3.00	0
66-67	Toronto	NHL	10	6	4	25	2.65	0
67-68	Los Angeles	NHL	5	2	3	18	3.86	1
68-69	Detroit	NHL						
69-70	New York	NHL	3	0	1	6	4.50	0
NHL POST-SEASON TOTALS			106	54	48	267	2.54	12

USHL Second All-Star Team: 47-48
USHL Top Rookie Award: 47-48
AHL Top Rookie Award: 48-49
AHL First All-Star Team: 49-50
NHL First All-Star Team: 50-51, 51-52, 52-53
NHL Second All-Star Team: 53-54, 54-55, 58-59, 62-63
NHL Calder Trophy (Top Rookie): 50-51
NHL Vezina Trophy Winner (Best Goaltender): 51-52, 52-53, 54-55, 64-65 (with Johnny Bower) Lester Patrick Trophy, awarded to player exemplifying dedication to hockey in the U.S.A., 1971 Inducted into the National Hockey League Hall of Fame, 1971

TIM MILES GILBERT HORTON

Position: Defenseman
Shoots: Right
Height: 5'10"
Weight: 180 lbs

Born: January 12, 1930
Cochrane, Ontario, Canada

Died: February 14, 1974
Toronto, Ontario, Canada

REGULAR SEASON

Year	Team	League	GP	G	A	PTS	P1M
46-47	Copper Cliff	NOHA	9	0	0	0	14
47-48	St. Mike's	OHA	32	6	7	13	137
48-49	St. Mike's	OHA	32	9	18	27	95
49-50	Toronto	NHL	1	0	0	0	2
50-51	Toronto	NHL	60	5	18	23	83
50-51	Pittsburgh	AHL	60	8	26	34	129
51-52	Toronto	NHL	4	0	0	0	8
51-52	Pittsburgh	AHL	64	12	19	31	146
52-53	Toronto	NHL	70	2	14	16	85
53-54	Toronto	NHL	70	7	24	31	94
54-55	Toronto	NHL	67	5	9	14	84
55-56	Toronto	NHL	35	0	5	5	36
56-57	Toronto	NHL	66	6	19	25	72
57-58	Toronto	NHL	53	6	20	26	39
58-59	Toronto	NHL	70	5	21	26	76
59-60	Toronto	NHL	70	3	29	32	69
60-61	Toronto	NHL	57	6	15	21	75
61-62	Toronto	NHL	70	10	28	38	88
62-63	Toronto	NHL	70	6	19	25	69
63-64	Toronto	NHL	70	9	20	29	71
64-65	Toronto	NHL	70	12	16	28	95
65-66	Toronto	NHL	70	6	22	28	76
66-67	Toronto	NHL	70	8	17	25	70
67-68	Toronto	NHL	69	4	23	27	82
68-69	Toronto	NHL	74	11	29	40	107
69-70	Toronto	NHL	59	3	19	22	91
	New York	NHL	15	1	5	6	16
70-71	New York	NHL	78	2	18	20	5
71-72	Pittsburgh	NHL	44	2	9	11	40
72-73	Buffalo	NHL	69	1	16	17	56
73-74	Buffalo	NHL	55	0	6	6	53
TWENTY-FOUR (24) NHL SEASONS			**1446**	**115**	**403**	**518**	**1611**

156

POST-SEASON

Year	Team	League	GP	G	A	PTS	PfM
46-47	Copper Cliff	NOHA	5	0	1	1	0
49-50	Toronto	NHL	1	0	0	0	2
50-51	Pittsburgh	AHL	13	0	9	9	16
51-52	Pittsburgh	AHL	11	1	3	4	16
53-54	Toronto	NHL	5	1	1	2	4
55-56	Toronto	NHL	2	0	0	0	4
58-59	Toronto	NHL	12	0	3	3	16
59-60	Toronto	NHL	10	0	1	1	6
60-61	Toronto	NHL	5	0	0	0	0
61-62	Toronto	NHL	12	3	13	16	16
62-63	Toronto	NHL	10	1	3	4	10
63-64	Toronto	NHL	14	0	4	4	20
64-65	Toronto	NHL	6	0	2	2	13
65-66	Toronto	NHL	4	1	0	1	12
66-67	Toronto	NHL	12	3	5	8	25
68-69	Toronto	NHL	4	0	0	0	7
69-70	New York	NHL	6	1	1	2	28
70-71	New York	NHL	13	1	4	5	14
71-72	Pittsburgh	NHL	4	0	1	1	2
72-73	Buffalo	NHL	6	0	1	1	4
NHL POST-SEASON TOTALS			**126**	**11**	**39**	**50**	**183**

AHL First Ali-Star Team: 51-52
NHL First All-Star Team: 63-64, 67-68, 68-69
NHL Second All-Star Team: 53-54, 62-63, 66-67
Inducted into National Hockey League Hall of Fame, 1977

PER-ERIK G. LINDBERGH

Position: Goaltender
Catches: Right
Height: 5' 9"
Weight: 160 lbs

Born: May 24, 1959
Stockholm, Sweden

Died: November 13, 1985
Philadelphia, Pennsylvania, U.S.A.

REGULAR SEASON

Year	Team	League	GP	W	L	T	GA	GAA	SO
79-80	AIK Elitserien	SEHL	31	14	13	4	106	3.43	1
	Team Sweden	Worlds	6				38	6.33	0
	Team Sweden	Pravo Cup	4				7	2.33	0
	Team Sweden	Izvestija Cup	4					4.50	0
80-81	Team Sweden	Olympics	5				18	3.60	
	Maine	AHL	51	31	14	5	165	3.26	2
81-82	Team Sweden	Canada Cup	2	0	2	0	8	4.00	2
	Maine	AHL	25	17	7	2	83	3.31	0
	Philadelphia	NHL	8	2	4	2	35	4.38	0
82-83	Philadelphia	NHL	40	23	13	3	116	2.98	3
	Team Sweden	Worlds	10				27	2.70	0
83-84	Philadelphia	NHL	36	16	13	3	135	4.05	1
	Springfield	AHL	4	4	0	0	12	3.00	0
84-85	Philadelphia	NHL	65	40	17	7	194	3.02	2
85-86	Philadelphia	NHL	8	6	2	0	23	2.88	1
FIVE 5 NHL SEASONS			**157**	**87**	**49**	**15**	**503**	**3.30**	**7**

POST-SEASON

Year	Team	League	GP	W	L	GA	GAA	SO
80-81	Maine	AHL	20	10	7	66	3.54	0
82-83	Philadelphia	NHL	3	0	3	18	6.00	0
83-84	Philadelphia	NHL	2	0	1	3	6.92	0
84-85	Philadelphia	NHL	18	12	6	42	2.50	0
NHL POST-SEASON TOTALS			**23**	**12**	**10**	**63**	**3.11**	**0**

AHL Hap Holmes Trophy Winner (Best Goalie): 80-81
AHL Most Valuable Player: 80-81 NHL All-Rookie Team: 82-83
NHL First All-Star Team: 84-85
NHL Vezina Trophy Winner (Best Goalie): 84-85

JOHN KORDIC

Position: Right Wing
Shoots: Right
Height: 5'11"
Weight: 225 lbs

Born: March 25, 1965
Edmonton, Alberta, Canada

Died: August 8, 1992
Quebec City, Quebec, Canada

REGULAR SEASON

Year	Team	League	GP	G	A	PTS	PIM
81-82	Edmonton	AHAA	42	1	16	17	78
82-83	Portland	WHL	72	3	17	22	235
	Portland	Mem. Cup	4	0	1	1	6
83-84	Portland	WHL	67	9	50	59	232
84-85	Portland	WHL	25	6	22	28	73
	Seattle	WHL	46	17	36	53	154
	Sherbrooke	AHL	4	0	0	0	4
85-86	Montreal	NHL	5	0	1	1	12
	Sherbrooke	AHL	68	3	14	17	238
87-88	Montreal	NHL	44	5	3	8	151
88-89	Montreal	NHL	6	0	0	0	13
	Toronto	NHL	46	1	2	3	185
89-90	Toronto	NHL	55	9	4	13	252
90-91	Toronto	NHL	3	0	0	0	9
	Newmarket	AHL	8	1	1	2	79
	Washington	NHL	7	0	0	0	101
91-92	Quebec	NHL	18	0	2	2	11
	Cape Breton	AHL	12	2	1	3	141
SEVEN (7) NHL SEASONS			**245**	**17**	**18**	**35**	**997**

POST-SEASON

Year	Team	League	GP	G	A	PTS	PIM
85-86	Montreal	NHL	18	0	0	0	53
86-87	Montreal	NHL	11	2	0	2	19
87-88	Montreal	NHL	7	2	2	4	26
88-89	Mtl-Toronto	NHL	-	-	-	-	-
89-90	Toronto	NHL	5	0	1	1	33
90-91	Tor-Wash	NHL	-	-	-	-	-
91-92	Quebec	NHL	-	-	-	-	-
NHL POST-SEASON TOTALS			**47**	**4**	**3**	**7**	**131**

WHL Second All-Star Team, 1984-85

STEVE CHIASSON

Position: Defenseman
Shoots: Left
Height: 6'1"
Weight: 205 lbs

Born: April 14, 1967
Barrie, Ontario, Canada

Died: May 3, 1999
Raleigh, North Carolina, U.S.A.

REGULAR SEASON

Year	Team	League	GP	G	A	PTS	PIM
84-85	Guelph	OHL	61	8	22	30	139
85-86	Guelph	OHL	54	12	41	42	126
86-87	Detroit	NHL	45	1	4	5	73
87-88	Detroit	NHL	29	2		11	57
88-89	Detroit	NHL	65	12	35	47	149
89-90	Detroit	NHL	67	14	28	42	114
90-91	Detroit	NHL	42	3	17	20	80
91-92	Detroit	NHL	62	10	24	34	136
92-93	Detroit	NHL	79	12	50	62	155
93-94	Detroit	NHL	82	13	33	46	122
94-95	Calgary	NHL	45	2	23	25	39
95-96	Calgary	NHL	76	8	25	33	62
96-97	Calgary	NHL	47	5	11	16	32
	Hartford	NHL	18	3	11	14	7
97-98	Carolina	NHL	66	7	27	34	65
98-99	Carolina	NHL	24	1	8	9	12
THIRTEEN (13) SEASONS			**503**	**61**	**212**	**273**	**634**

POST-SEASON

Year	Team	League	GP	G	A	PTS	PIM
85--86	Guelph	OHL	18	10	10	20	37
86-87	Detroit	NHL	2	0	0	0	19
87-88	Detroit	NHL	9	2	2	4	31
88-89	Detroit	NHL	5	2	1	3	6
90-91	Detroit	NHL	5	3	1	4	19
91-92	Detroit	NHL	11	1	5	6	12
92-93	Detroit	NHL	7	2	2	4	19
93-94	Detroit	NHL	7	2	3	5	2
94-95	Calgary	NHL	7	1	2	3	9
95-96	Calgary	NHL	4	2	1	3	0
98-99	Carolina	NHL	6	1	2	3	10
NHL POST-SEASON TOTALS			**63**	**16**	**19**	**35**	**127**

Stafford Smythe Trophy Winner (Memorial Cup Tournament Most Valuable Player): 85-86
Memorial Cup First All-Star Team: 85-86
Played in 1993 NHL All-Star Game

CPSIA information can be obtained
at www.ICGtesting.com
Printed in the USA
FSOW02n1944251115
13915FS